The Ultimate

Your Self Revealed

Other Writings by Marie S. Watts

The Ultimate	published 1957
Just Be Your Self	1957
Your Eternal Identity	1958
Prayers and Excerpts from The Word	1961
Success Is Normal	1963
You Are the Splendor	1966
Gems from The Word, Booklet 1	1966
Gems from The Word, Booklet 2	1970
Gems from The Word, Booklet 3	1971
Poems of The Ultimate	1971
The Gospel of Thomas	

Classnotes

Three Essential Steps	1959
Fulfillment of Purpose, Vol. 1	1965
Fulfillment of Purpose, Vol. 2	1965
The Omnipresent I Am, Vol. 1	1966
The Omnipresent I Am, Evidenced, Vol. 2	1967
The Ultimate Awareness, an Eternal Constant, Vol. 1	1969
The Ultimate Awareness, an Eternal Constant, Vol. 2	1969

These and other books by Marie S. Watts
Are available through:
Mystics of the World
Eliot, Maine
www.mysticsoftheworld.com

The Ultimate

Your Self Revealed

Marie S. Watts

The Ultimate

Mystics of the World First Edition 2015
Published by Mystics of the World
ISBN-13: 978-0692384343
ISBN-10: 0692384340

For information contact:
Mystics of the World
Eliot, Maine
www.mysticsoftheworld.com

Cover graphics by Margra Muirhead
Printed by CreateSpace
Available from Mystics of the World and Amazon.com

Marie S. Watts

Originally published 1957

Contents

Chapter I
GOD 15
Chapter II
TRUTH 24
Chapter III
MIND 33
Chapter IV
FREEDOM 45
Chapter V
IDENTITY 53
Chapter VI
BODY 69
Chapter VII
BEAUTY 89
Chapter VIII
LIFE ETERNAL 96
Chapter IX
NO KARMA 104
Chapter X
LOVE 110
Chapter XI
GREATER WORKS 116
CHAPTER XII
SEEING IS BEING 144
Chapter XIII
THY NAME 149

Chapter XIV

   THE ULTIMATE 153

About the Author 155

Introduction

What are the universal questions that rise from the hearts of all of us? Are they not *who* are we? *What* are we? *Why* are we? Do we not all question, at some point in this human journey, what brings us into our present experience? Do we not all, at some time, ask ourselves, "Why am I here? What is the purpose?"

In this book, *The Ultimate,* the author brings a revelatory approach to these questions of *Who? What?* and *Why?* In clear and cogent terms, she cuts through the entanglements of wishful thinking and sets forth the answers that have come to her in revelation and in proof through her years of consecrated study of the workings of divine Principle. Here, also, her approach to the subject of "body" casts new light upon something that has been a stumbling block in many a metaphysical treatise.

The Ultimate is a challenging title. But the challenge lies in the semantics of that term as it filters through the varying shades of interpretation in the mind of the reader. Perhaps the author best sets forth its true import when she says, "This Ultimate permits no deviation from the one central fact that God is *all* that exists in the universe, including that which we call man."

As one studies this book and begins to accept its statements, the challenge disappears. Then begins a new alignment of values with consequent unfoldment. Then comes a new meaning of *identity* and with it the realization of what we really are and what our true destiny is.

The author has had to prove every step of the way. From her childhood, there was always the longing to know God. In later years, as each unfoldment came, she yearned to share with others the fruits of her knowing, even when the time was not yet ripe.

At one time, music seemed to hold an answer. She became a concert artist. But no measure of outward success satisfied the constant query, "What is God, and how may I know Him?" She eventually became a teacher of considerable note in the music field, but the search for the Light became more intensive with each advance.

Step by step, her quest brought her into the service of healing. She was to know the joy of witnessing ruptured family ties reunited, insanity give place to sanity, and victims of so called incurable diseases restored to active and purposeful living.

As a sequence to this experience came her publication *Just Be Yourself*. In this booklet she states, "If we continue on in this quiet exploration of God as *all* the Life that lives," she says that we will learn that healing, as we speak of it, is actually better termed "the revelation of that perfection which has always existed."

To those earnestly seeking freedom from the complexities and pressures of this changing human pattern and wishing to learn more of their true identity, this book will provide a stimulating and rewarding answer.

Gertrude M. New

Foreword

What is the Ultimate? At first glance, the title to this book, *The Ultimate,* may seem to present a challenge, or it could appear presumptuous. However, the answer to the above question will disclose that neither of these attitudes is implied.

The Ultimate is that glorious point in revelation where the long struggle for spiritual understanding is ended, where ever-present perfection is realized to be the entirety of the Life, Soul, Being, and Body of the seeker. Of course, this does not mean that all revelation has come to an end. Rather it is from this point that *the Truth reveals Itself from within* in ever-increasing light and clarity. Here you stand *in* the Light *as* the Light; and the Light is Consciousness — *your Consciousness.*

In the Ultimate there is no dualism. Here there is conscious awareness that God is *in* the universe *as* the universe. God is recognized to be the Life, Mind, Soul, substance, and body of all that has existence. This infinite Self-containment includes *you,* your entire Life, Mind, Soul, substance, being, body, and experience.

Standing *in* the Light *as* the Light, you have reached the point of expansion. Without further seeking and without mental effort, your conscious awareness of your spiritual identity constantly expands in glorious Self-revelation. You know as you are known because you know as the Mind that was in Christ Jesus, the Mind that is God. "Let this mind be in you, which was also in Christ Jesus" (Phil. 2:5).

In the Ultimate, your Self is revealed in Its eternal, changeless perfection. Beyond all the spurious claims of beginning, changing, or ending —of birth, age, or death—you abide in conscious peace, perfection, and security. "There remaineth therefore a rest to the people of God" (Heb. 4:9).

Here you know God, you experience God; and in this Consciousness you know and experience your Self. Why? *Because God, identified, individualized, and expressed, is your Self.* Every truth presented in this book is the existing fact of your Self. The Mind that has expressed Its truth here is the Mind that reads and recognizes this truth to be true. This is your Mind in glad Self-recognition. Your inner response to the Ultimate is your inherent awareness that this is your own truth because it is the fact of your existence.

This conscious Self-revelation will not take place by a casual reading of this book. Neither will it become apparent by a mental struggle to understand the truth presented here. It will appear as you *persist* in a calm, quiet contemplation of the Self-revealing Ultimate.

Sometimes this question arises, "Will this heal me or solve my problems?" The answer is, "No!" What does happen is this: you discover that you have never been out of the kingdom of God and that the kingdom of God has ever been established *in* and *as* your entire Being. Furthermore, the perfection you have been seeking is perceived to be the eternally established *fact* of your existence; therefore, there is nothing in need of healing, and there are no problems to be solved. Instead of working on a problem which does *not* exist, you see through it to the present perfection which *does* exist.

Dear reader, this revelation of the Ultimate is not just a beautiful theory. It is Truth revealed; and when Truth is revealed, perfection is always realized. You do not struggle to become that conscious Perfection which you already are; neither do you strive to overcome an imperfection which you are not. You perceive, without effort, the eternal, changeless nature of your Life, Soul, Being, and Body.

In my booklet, *Just Be Yourself,* I have related the experience which first revealed to me the glorious power of the realization of the allness of God. Throughout the intervening years, that revelation has continued to expand. Again and again, I have seen this omnipotent Truth prove Itself in revealing perfection where imperfection had presented an appearance that would claim to be alarming or, at times, even fatal.

The Truth, as presented in *The Ultimate,* has gradually revealed Itself through many instances of just such proofs, as well as through countless nights and days of study, meditation, questioning, and above all, listening for the answers to these questions. Sometimes the answers have been simultaneous with the questions; at other times, I have asked the same questions over and over again. But invariably that still, small, inner Voice has answered, and I have *known* and recognized It to be God *reminding me of that which I already knew.*

The Truth is no more true for one than for another. The Truth revealed in these pages is true *for* you, is true *of* you, and, above all, is true *as you*.

Beloved, this is the gift of God. This is God's gift of Himself. Accept it and walk in freedom, strength, and joy unspeakable.

Chapter I

GOD

I am come that they might have life,
and that they might have it more abundantly.
—John 10:10

This is a *book of Life*, your Life. Within these pages, you are destined to become acquainted with your Self. Here you will discover your Life, Mind, Being, and Body as you are, as you have ever been, and as you will forever continue to be. This you that you are, as set forth here, is far too important to be passed over lightly or read about in a casual manner. Therefore, this is not a book to be read desultorily and then tucked away on the library shelf. Rather it is a textbook to be studied, a reference book to be kept at hand as a constant reminder of what you are, when illusion presents a false picture of what you are not. While you study the Truth as presented here, thoughtfully, meditatively, you will exclaim, "Why, this is true of me. I am this Truth. I AM THAT I AM, and I know it."

In starting on this voyage of Self-discovery, there is one paramount fact, one all-important truth it is necessary to know: that God is All *as all. Any attempt to perceive the Ultimate* Reality without this conscious realization is futile and can lead only to confusion, contradiction, and frustration. Often, sincere students along the spiritual way become discouraged and fail to attain the high goal they have set for themselves. The reason is this: they have not fully and completely understood or accepted God *as* All. In order to arrive at complete perception of Reality, it is necessary to accept completely God, Reality. There can be no qualified or partial acceptance of this Truth. It must be a full and complete acceptance without qualifications or reservations.

So let us repeat: God is All *as* all. God is the universe and all it contains. God is infinite, eternal, limitless, and immeasurable in terms of time and space. Without beginning, without ending, without change or duplication, *God is.* All existence, all consciousness of existence is God. All Life, Substance, Form, Activity, Love, Intelligence comprise God. There is nothing beside or outside of the *one all infinite Presence* which is God.

Indeed, there is no outside, as the infinitude of God is *All.* All that is contained in this infinitude is God — the Allness, the Oneness, the Onliness of all that has existence. God is omnipresent and Omnipresence; there is nothing present, no Presence, but God. God is omniactive and Omniaction; there is no action, and none active, but God. God is omnipotent and Omnipotence; there is no power in operation, and no power existing, but God. God is omniscient and Omni-science; there is nothing known, and no mind to know anything, but God-Mind. If you will accept this truth completely, without qualification or reservation, and will hold to it steadfastly, you are indeed well along on your way to Self-discovery.

Just about now, you may be wondering why all this emphasis is being placed on the omni-presence, the omnipotence, and the omniscience of God. The answer is simple. The first requisite in knowing your Self, in Self-knowledge, is to *know God*. When you know what God is, really know and experience God, you will know what you are and will experience being that glorious Self. You will experience a *perfect Self*, forever joyous and free. Why is this? Because God is what you are and all that exists as you.

Jesus knew this perfectly. In John 10:15 we read, "As the Father knoweth me, even so know I the Father." And all of us remember that conversation between the Master and Philip in John 14:8-9:

> Philip saith unto him, Lord, shew us the Father, and it sufficeth us. Jesus saith unto him, Have I been so long time with you, and yet hast thou not known me, Philip? he that hath seen me hath seen the Father; and how sayest thou then, Shew us the Father?

Glorious words of Truth, and we are just now beginning to realize their full import. There are many passages in the Bible revealing the presence of God *as* Jesus. There are also passages setting forth the truth that we—you and I—are included *in and as that Presence.* As you continue on through this book, these truths as given in the Bible will be set forth and explained.

There is a word in the English language, one of the very short words, too, that has been almost overlooked in the metaphysical world. That little word is *as.* We have heard and read much about the fact that God is All-in-all, that God is in the universe; but we never hear or read that God is All *as* all; that God exists *as* the universe, *as* you and me, and *as* all that has life, form, mind, or activity.

You can readily see that unless we perceive that God is All *as* all, we will have to accept a presence and a power apart from God. This is dualism, a house divided against itself; thus, it invariably leads to confusion and ends in failure. Dualism is the stumbling block for many sincere students of Truth. It is easy to understand why this should seem to be a difficult hurdle for anyone. The world, *as it appears,* is so extremely contradictory to the Perfection we know God to be.

Let us now begin to see through that contradiction. The universe, planets, and the world *do* exist, and they are real. You and I, everyone and everything having life, form, mind, and activity, are genuine. It is folly to pretend that the universe and all it contains are nothing. So let us acknowledge their presence and then *intelligently know just what we are acknowledging.*

To one who has not yet attained spiritual perception, the universe, the world, *appears* to be composed of matter, air, and material elements. The universe also *appears* to be controlled by a power that can operate either constructively or destructively. It *appears* to have had beginning, to be constantly changing, and to be hastening toward its own destruction or ending. All of us are familiar, too familiar, with these false appearances.

Having stated what the universe appears to be—*and is not*—let us now perceive what it *is*. In this, as in all quests for Truth, we turn to the allness of God. "Do not I fill heaven and earth? saith the Lord" (Jer. 23: 24). Indeed, God does fill heaven and earth. The universe, infinity, is God, and all it contains is God's infinite Self-containment. God is *in* the All *as* the All. Now we have arrived at the point where we must know the nature of God.

Among the many synonyms for God, we find the following: Spirit, Mind, Life, Love. So let us begin with Spirit. To many, the term *Spirit* is almost meaningless, or at best, it has a very vague connotation. It appears to them as intangible, nebulous, devoid of substance, form, or activity.

If this were true, Spirit, God, would be without evidence of His own existence. What evidence of existence would we have without substance, form, or activity? None.

God, Spirit, *is* existence and *is* evident, manifest as spiritual substance, form, and activity right here and now. This universe—its substance, form, and activity—*is* real, tangible, genuine, as Spirit. To those who spiritually perceive, *the only reality, the only existence, is in and as Spirit.*

Yes, this universe, where you live and move and have your being, is entirely Spirit. All that we have been misinterpreting as material substance, form, is *here*; but it is not here as matter. Rather it exists as eternal, perfect, immutable Spirit. There is nothing wrong with *this* universe. The only thing wrong is the way we have been seeing and interpreting it.

We have been seeing a distortion of that which is—a mirage instead of that which really does exist.

Those who have experienced spiritual illumination know this to be true. God, Spirit, really *is* All and is manifest *as* all. But Spirit can only be manifest, be evident, as Spirit. If this seems difficult to understand or accept, ponder this verse from Hebrews 11:1: "Now faith is the substance of things hoped for, the evidence of things not seen." Have faith—not a blind faith but an intelligent conviction—that the truths you have been reading and repeating are really true. A calm, confident persistence in this kind of faith reveals the substance we have been hoping to behold and the evidence of the universe of Spirit that we have not seen so long as we have been "seeing through a glass, darkly."

Yes, Spirit is omnipresent; but Mind, Life, Truth, Love, and all that God *is* must be included in Omnipresence. Otherwise God would be incomplete. Wherever God is—and He is everywhere—*He is in His entirety*. In other words, all that God is exists equally throughout infinity and eternity. God as Spirit includes God as Mind, Life, Soul, Principle. The use of any one of the synonyms for God must imply the presence of all that God is. Omnipotence, Omnipresence, Omniaction, Omniscience are all synonyms for God. They are not separable, one from the other. Neither can they be excluded from the totality of all that God is. Thus, you can see that the presence of God is the power of God, the mind of God, the intelligence of God, the eternal life of God, and the love of God.

It is this realization of the all-inclusiveness of God that enables you to see through any seeming problem, whether it might appear to be mental or physical; whether it presents itself as a threat to life or as any other phase of apparent discord. Of course, our all-absorbing theme must ever be the allness, the onliness of God. But in specific appearance of discord, it is helpful to contemplate just what God is as Mind, as Life, or as whatever the truth of what God *is*, instead of the appearance of what God *is not*.

Yes, the universe and all it contains is God. And that which comprises God is the essence, the substance, the activity, the intelligence, and the form of *all that is formed*. Just as God is eternal, beginningless, endless, changeless existence, so all that God exists *as* remains forever in its eternal, immutable state of perfection. God is not subject to chance or change. God is not subject to disintegration, destruction, or distortion. God is not subject to the pangs of birth or the throes of death. Neither does He know Himself nor can He be known as subject to any of these falsities. Nothing is ever added to or taken from the allness of God.

This is truth. How can it be otherwise, when God is—and knows Himself to be—the substance, life, form, mind of all existence as Himself? God really *is* the only Mind. He *is* the one Mind that knows, and He *is* the entire essence, substance, form, and activity of that which He knows.

Reader, do you ask how this pertains to you? Do you wonder in just what way this is going to help you in solving some seeming problem? Let me assure you of one thing: *this is the only way*. In this way you will discover that you have no problem to solve. It will be revealed to you that *only that which is true of God is true of you.* Indeed, you exist as the very presence of what God is. And there is nothing present in you or in your experience but God. The Mind that is God knows no unsolved problems. And what Mind could identify Itself as your Mind other than the only Mind, God-Mind?

Does this seem obscure to you? Does it seem impractical or impossible? If so, ask yourself this question: "In my affirmations that God is the only Mind, the only Life, have I really believed what I was saying?" If your answer is in the affirmative, it will not be difficult for you to perceive the simplicity, the unequivocal rightness of this Absolute Truth. In Ecclesiastes 3:15, we find this inspired statement of the Ultimate: "That which hath been is now; and that which is to be hath already been; and God requireth that which is past."

> Dear reader, it must be clear to you now that the allness, the entirety, the totality of God includes you. You—your life, mind, body, being—are included in the changeless perfection of God, the All *as* the all.

Chapter II

TRUTH

What is truth?

—*John 18:38*

Nearly two thousand years ago Pontius Pilate asked Jesus this all-important question. We have no record that Jesus answered Pilate. Why didn't he? Probably because he knew that his answer would neither be understood nor believed.

The search for the answer to this question has continued and is still continuing today. Yet Jesus *did* give the answer. Clearly and simply, he stated, "I am the truth." Why wasn't it understood? It was just too simple. He could just as well have said to Pilate, "*You* are the truth, if you only knew it."

A clear perception of the teachings of the Master will disclose that he did not claim the exclusive right or privilege of being the Truth. Neither did he limit that prerogative to his immediate disciples. In John 14:12 we read: "He that believeth on me, the works that I do shall he do also; and greater works than these shall he do." Certain it is that Jesus was not speaking of himself as a person. Hadn't he referred to himself repeatedly as the impersonal Life, Truth, and

24

Way? In the following prayer, one of the most beautiful ever recorded, we find Jesus praying that all of us may recognize the truth—one God as the *I* of each of us:

> That they all may be one; as thou, Father, art in me, and I in thee, that they also may be one in us ... I in them, and thou in me, that they may be made perfect in one (John 17:21, 23).

The fact that this prayer is all-inclusive is indicated in the following verse, John 17:20: "Neither pray I for these alone, but for them also which shall believe on me through their word." Does this sound as though Jesus spoke of himself as the Truth to the exclusion of all others?

Who or what is the *I* referred to in the foregoing passages? Who is the "me" in whom we are asked to believe? There is but one *I,* the *I* that exists as the identity of you, of me, and of each and every one of us. And this is the *I,* the *Me,* we are asked to believe in. Yes, my friends, we are exhorted to accept, to acknowledge, the *I* that is the impersonal Truth, the *I* that *I* am, as the identity of each of us.

Again and again we have been assured that if we would just "know the truth," we would be made free. But how can we know anything unless we *perceive the nature* of that which we are knowing? When we know anything, really know it, that knowledge is forever present in, or as, our very consciousness, our mind. Thus, we discover that we actually include and *are* that which we know. In other words, it is impossible to know fully the truth until we become aware that *we are the very truth we are knowing.*

Again, what is truth? The truth of anything is the established fact of that which constitutes its existence. A dictionary definition includes this interpretation: "That which is true; a real state of things; fact; actuality." Yes, *truth is the fact of that which exists as the universe, the world, and as you and me.* Truth is eternal, without beginning, change, or ending. Being infinite, eternal, truth is forever harmonious and perfect.

The perception of the exact nature of truth is of vital importance to all of us. Why? *Because the truth is the established fact, the reality of all that exists.* To know the truth is to be conscious of the changeless perfection that constitutes the entirety of the universe; and that entirety includes you, me, and everyone. When we can know the truth with the same assurance that we know that two ones make two, and with no more effort, we are really *knowing the truth.*

Often we have thought that we were knowing the truth, when all we were doing was indulging in wishful thinking. Really to know anything is to be conscious of its immutable, established existence; to include that knowledge in our consciousness to such an extent that it could never occur to us that it could be any other than as it is.

The established fact that one plus one equals two includes no condition, no partial truth. In the same way, the basic truth that the one, all, immutable, eternal, perfect God comprises the entirety of existence can never include a part, a condition, or an opposite.

Frequently we have known the truth as though in opposition to something, as though there were certain forces opposing truth. The road of affirmations and denials leads us into this fallacy. If something could exist in opposition to truth, it would mean that truth was not the whole and complete fact of the reality, of that which has existence. A denial of error never reveals truth. Neither does it make truth any more true than It is this instant. We are never concerned with that which is not true because it is nonexistent. *Why dwell on nothing?* Rather, we contemplate the basic fact of existence—the allness, the onliness, the unbroken, uninterrupted, omnipotent, omnipresent presence of Perfection, *which does exist.*

Dear reader, does it seem to you that we are dwelling too long on this subject of truth? If so, be a little patient, for you will presently discover that *You* are the very Truth that is being presented here. Remember this: the Master recognized himself to be the Truth, and that is the same Self-recognition that is beginning to take place in you.

Just about now, you may be reflecting, "But this is all so intangible. How can I possibly be this Truth?"

Do you remember that in the beginning of this message we stated that the universe in which you live and move and have your being is the real universe, the *only* universe? You, the you that exists right here and now, is the real you, the *only* You in existence. God is the entirety, the all, of the universe, and that allness, that entirety, includes you. *That which is true of God as the universe is true of you because you are included in the Allness, the Onliness, of God.* The basic fact, truth, of omnipresent, omnipotent Perfection is the established truth of your perfection. Now do you perceive the vital importance of a clear concept of *all* that comprises Truth?

Another aspect of truth is the fact that It never has beginning, end, or change. Sometimes we postpone our realization of present perfection by working for something to *become* true. Truth never becomes true. Neither does falsity become untrue. Truth has always been true, and falsity has always been untrue, nonexistent. It is as simple as that.

It is in dwelling on the omnipresence of Perfection that Perfection is realized. It is in this way that the truth that is true about you becomes apparent as the Truth that is true *as* you. It is in this way that we attain Self-awareness, Self-consciousness. There is One Self only, and that is God, the One All-inclusive Self. It makes no difference how many distinct identities this Self includes, the fact remains that *God is the entirety of each identity*. It must be clear to you now that there can be nothing true, *a genuine fact* about you, that is not included in the Truth that is God.

Yes, God is eternally All and unconditionally perfect. An unconditioned fact is complete as its own truth. You are the Truth — *the unconditioned, eternally, perfect One identified as You*. This is a statement of the absolute, ultimate truth of your entire existence, life, mind, body, and being. This Truth, *as You*, is unqualified, unopposed, unconditioned. You are not dual. There are not two of you. There is no such thing as a You that is this Truth and another you that is the direct opposite of the perfect One which has always been, will ever be, You.

You may now be asking, "But what about this body? How can I reconcile this truth of Perfection with this suffering, sick, aging body?" You can't. You don't. *Never can you reconcile truth with untruth.* Be assured, though, that you *do* have a body. It is not the body that you have been mistaken about but the *kind of body* you have been misidentifying as your body.

This subject of body is of tremendous importance and will be gone into thoroughly in a later chapter in this book. For the time being, it is sufficient to know that, as you include your body, all that is discovered to be the truth, fact, about you is the established truth about your body.

The world, as it appears, is in a constant state of change. Everything, everyone, is seemingly in a temporal state. Non-existence is supposed to change into existence, life; while existence, life, is supposed to change into non-existence, death. Even the substances of the earth are supposed to be constantly changing into something else. The spurious evidence is constantly one of creating, changing, maturing, dissolving, deteriorating, and destroying. In the universe of appearance, nothing is established as eternal. There is always an arriving at or a going from some condition. In fact, the only thing that appears permanent in this false concept of the universe is change.

> The very nature of change, in this false view of reality, is proof that it is not true. Why? *Because Truth does not change.* God is Truth, and God is forever immutable.

Anything that appears to have beginning, change, or ending is not Truth, and therefore, not an established fact. Birth, maturing, changing, and dying are all aspects of this illusory distortion of *that which actually exists.*

Again, Truth stands established as It is and always has been. Have you ever noticed this? When some erroneous condition of body appears to be healed, the body remains. All that disappears is the inharmonious picture. What does this signify? It can only mean that anything in the nature of inharmony, anything that is added or changed, is false. If we could only realize the full import of this truth, we would then be aware of the eternality of body as well as of Mind, Life, and Spirit.

Yes, that which is Truth, that which is Reality —and there is no unreality—is the changeless fact of that which exists. Truth never began to be true. Truth never stopped being Truth. Nothing is ever added to It, and nothing is ever subtracted from It. Truth is never in a state of becoming, nor in a state of disappearing. It is eternal, changeless fact, an eternal existent.

With what mind do you know the Truth? God is the only Mind; so what mind is it that doesn't know the Truth? God, Mind, is eternally aware of the beginningless, changeless, endless nature of His existence. *You can have no Mind other than God-Mind, for there is no other.* This Mind that is conscious of being forever changelessly perfect, identified as You, is your Mind. There are no interruptions and no vacuums in the knowing, the conscious awareness of this Mind.

God, Mind, being conscious of the truth of His eternal perfection, is this instant identified as your Mind being conscious of your change-less perfection. *In other words, you are conscious Perfection being consciously perfect.*

31

This is the truth about you. This is the Truth *as* you. This is what Jesus meant when He said, "I am the truth." This is a true statement of the immutable, continuously perfect nature of your entire Being and the entirety of everyone existing.

How do you perceive this to be true of you? *Accept it; acknowledge it; claim your identity as it.* Know that the truth that makes you free is the truth that you *are* free.

> Calmly and persistently contemplate the established truth of your Being, and you will presently discover that this Truth is established *as your Being*. This is the way. Walk ye in it.

Chapter III

MIND

For God hath not given us the spirit of fear;
but of power, and of love, and of a sound mind.
—II Tim. 1:7

What is this gift of a sound mind that God has given us? It is the gift of Himself, the gift of His own Mind, His own Consciousness. In the perception of this truth, there is infinite power, infinite freedom from fear, and infinite love, peace, and security. Every so-called healing that has ever taken place has been omnipotent, omnipresent Mind aware of Its constant perfection. The manifestation of perfection may seem to appear through the understanding of a person, a practitioner, friend, or at times yourself. But this is only the appearance.

The mind of the practitioner and the mind of the one seeking help is *one and the same Mind* —and that Mind is God.

This is apparent from the fact that so-called absent treatments are effective. Actually, there is no such thing as an absent treatment. Omnipresent Mind is indivisible Mind, which is never absent.

God is Mind. There is one God; thus, there is one Mind. The Mind that is God is never divided, is never parceled out, but forever remains complete in Its oneness, Its allness. There are not minds many, neither are there personal minds. Rather there is the One Mind, as the Mind of you, the Mind of me, the Mind of everyone. There is no personal mind, no mortal or material mind, and no human mind. There is no such thing as *a mind of your own* functioning independently and of itself. The only Mind in existence is God-Mind, and this Mind belongs to God and to God alone. This is the Mind that is individualized, identified right here and now as your individual, identical Mind. *This is the Mind that is writing these words, and this is the Mind that is reading them.*

Never believe for a moment that what is termed the human mind could perceive or understand this truth. All of us are acquainted with those to whom this truth appears false, even ridiculous. As to this, we can only say that the Mind that is Truth recognizes Its own truth as Itself. Actually, there is no Mind not knowing truth. Non-recognition of truth would mean absence of Mind, total ignorance, darkness, a complete void. As infinite Mind is omnipresent, this absence of Mind is impossible.

Again and again, practitioners have heard some such statement as the following: "Oh, I know all of this intellectually, in theory, but I can't prove it." (The words may vary, but the meaning remains the same.) Do you know that such a statement is a denial of the very Mind that is conscious of the truth? You may be assured of one thing: the Mind that recognizes, admits, acknowledges the truth is the Mind that is God being conscious of His own truth. The mere fact that you are attracted to and in agreement with Truth is proof that you are seeing and knowing as the Mind that is God. *Indeed, no one would be on this path unless the Mind that is God were already functioning as the Mind of this one.*

With this realization, all seeming barriers are dissolved, and the glorious Light dawns. The false sense of having to prove something evaporates in the awareness that *all is God; all is perfect now.* Instantaneous perfection is manifest, and we call it healing. There is no gap, no separation between Mind's consciousness of Its perfection and the manifestation of that perfection. *Conscious perfection is manifest perfection.* That is why Jesus could speak "and it was done." He knew that he was speaking and acting as the Mind that is God.

It is God's joy and pleasure to individualize Itself as you and me and to function as us. "For it is God which worketh in you both to will and to do of his good pleasure" (Phil 2:13). "It is your Father's good pleasure to give you the kingdom" (Luke 12:32).

Always remember, *there are not two minds —* one knowing the truth and the other not knowing it. There is one Mind, one Consciousness, one awareness, and this conscious awareness is present right here and now as your conscious awareness. There is no unexpressed, unidentified Mind. It is impossible that Mind could be inactive, meaningless, or purposeless. Indeed, the very function of Mind is to express Itself, identify Itself, individualize Itself.

No one can doubt that the governing Principle of the entire universe is intelligence. This all-intelligent Mind is the Mind that is actively functioning as your Mind, governing you, all your affairs and experiences. You never have to prove it. The mere fact, truth, of it being true is its own proof. Your only necessity is to accept it without reservation or qualification. In this way only will you know fully what it means to say, "I and my Father are one."

Is Mind conscious, aware of Itself as you? Yes. Wherever Mind is—and It is everywhere—It is conscious of Itself as being. How do you know that Mind is conscious of Itself *as* you? You are conscious of yourself. You are aware that you exist. With what other mind could you be aware of your existence? Just as you are conscious of yourself, your identity, so God is conscious of existing *as* you, as your identity—as the entirety of your life, mind, substance, activity, and experience. In other words:

> Your consciousness of yourself as existing
> is God being conscious of Itself existing as you.

All that is ever known is contained within the entirety of God, Mind. It is impossible that God could know anything outside of, or other than, Himself. There is no outside; neither is there anything other than God to be known. Anything other than omnipotent, omnipresent Perfection is utter nothingness, non-existence. Even God could have no knowledge of anything that was entirely without existence.

What does Mind know about Itself? First of all, It knows Its allness, Its all-inclusive entirety, Its oneness. Consciousness is forever cognizant of Its eternality, immutability, perfection. Here there is no awareness of birth, change, or death. Never having had beginning, Mind can know no beginning; being eternal by virtue of Its very nature, It can know no ending. Being forever immutable, It can know no change. In short, Consciousness can only be aware of Itself. In this Mind, there is, therefore, no awareness of sickness, age, decay, deterioration, or changing activity. No suffering and no sufferer are known here, and no evil or evildoer is contained within God's infinite Self-knowledge.

Mind is never impoverished. Within Its infinite Self-containment, all that It can ever desire eternally exists. Every right desire and the conscious power of fulfillment of that desire are contained within this all-knowing Mind. There is no separation between desire and fruition. *Mind is One.* This fact precludes any possibility of an absence of the manifestation at the *instant* the need or desire arises. It makes no difference whether the need may appear to be for health, money, home, activity, or whatever, the need and the supply are one. They appear simultaneously, and there is no gap in either time or space between them.

Actually, there is neither time nor space, as we shall discover in our study of this book. Everything that has ever been true is true right now. Everything that is ever going to be true is true in this very instant. Everything that is true now is known now, and the knowing, the perception, and the manifestation are one this instant. "The thing that hath been, it is that which shall be; and that which is done is that which shall be done: and there is no new thing under the sun" (Eccles. 1:9).

What Mind is it that knows all this? Your Mind, the only Mind there is, individualized, identified as your identical Mind. When? Right now, this very instant. There is tremendous power in this realization. That which the world terms miracles takes place when this Light fully dawns.

That is what Jesus saw when the loaves and fishes were multiplied. The need, then and there, was not for money. Rather it was for food, and the food was right there where and when it was needed. When the need was for tax money, it was found to be right there in the mouth of a fish. When it was for health, wholeness, or healing of any kind, that is exactly what was supplied instantly. Why? Because the supply was all that had ever been there. Never had there been a lack, either of health or wealth. *Not one thing was changed. It was simply that their eyes were opened and they perceived that which had always been the truth.*

Suppose, for instance, the immediate need is for protection. Read again what took place when the servant of Elisha was frightened:

> And when the servant of the man of God was risen early, and gone forth, behold, an host compassed the city both with horses and chariots. And his servant said unto him, Alas my master! how shall we do?
> And he answered, Fear not: for they that be with us are more than they that be with them.
> And Elisha prayed, and said, Lord, I pray thee, open his eyes, that he may see. And the Lord opened the eyes of the young man; and he saw: and, behold, the mountain was full of horses and chariots of fire round about Elisha (2 Kings 6:15-17).

There was no delay, no running for protection. The protection was needed—the protection was realized instantly.

What is the source from which all this omni-present supply appears? *You are.* Just as surely as you have existence, you are conscious. You can only be conscious *as* the One Consciousness which comprises all that exists. You could not be conscious as another, for there is no other Mind or Consciousness. *As this Mind, you produce from your own consciousness the instant supply for every need.* Why haven't you proved this? Because you have not perceived your identity as Mind identified *as* You. Really, the seeming lack of this perception has only been taking place in this mistaken sense of identity. It hasn't been going on in you at all.

Mind does not prey upon Itself. The author discovered the power of this realization many years ago. Immediately after moving into a new neighborhood, the house became infested with ants. Upon inquiry, it was discovered that this was the situation in the entire neighborhood. Nothing had been found that would eradicate them perma-nently.

At first, the thought came that those ants were an expression of Life; thus, they must have their place but that their place was not in this home. The ants remained. Something more had to be perceived. Then the revelation appeared:

Infinite Mind is all that can express Itself, manifest Itself, or be conscious of Itself as existing. It is impossible that omnipotent Mind could appear, manifest, as something inimical to Its own peace and harmony. Neither is it possible that Mind could express Itself as Life, activity, substance, or form of a parasitical nature. Mind does not prey upon Itself, and It has no awareness of anything that can prey upon It.

Overnight the ants disappeared. No trace of them was ever found in that home again, although they continued to plague the neighbors.

What Mind knew this truth? Could a puny, assumptive mortal or human mind have had that glorious, powerful revelation? No! That revelation was the Mind that is God revealing Itself to Itself. *It was conscious Perfection being consciously perfect.*

For years we have spoken about Mind *and* Its manifestation. No one can doubt that the discovery of this great truth has been a tremendous help to many sincere students of metaphysics. Yet the full power of this truth is not realized until it is revealed that Mind exists *as* manifestation. All that has life, substance, form, or activity is Mind manifesting *as that which It is.* Mind, Life, Substance, Being are not separate. They are One, and this One is eternal, forever conscious of Its perfection.

Mind is not suicidal. Neither is It Self-destructive. Mind is *all* that is manifest, and *It can manifest nothing other than that which It is.* Does Mind contain within Itself an element capable of destroying Its own substance, life, existence? Could Mind manifest Itself as a parasitical growth that would prey upon Its embodiment of Itself? Could eternal Mind manifest as something that would bring Its existence to an end? Could omnipotent, omniactive Mind manifest Its activity in a way that would cause that activity to come to an end? No, never can any of these impossibles be, or become, possible.

Dear reader, is it becoming clear to you that you—your entire Mind, body, activity, experience —are the very presence and power of this Mind? You are this Mind identified, individualized, manifest *as* you. All that you have, all that you are, all that you are conscious of having or being is this Mind, conscious of Itself, identified *as* You. The author could tell you of seeming miracles taking place through this realization.

You *are* just what you know—*and nothing else.* There are not two of you—one knowing and the other not knowing. In order to exist at all, you must exist *as* this Mind. In order to be conscious at all, you must be conscious *as* this Consciousness. Yes, even to be alive, you must be alive *as* this Life. Only God-Life lives. Only God-Mind is conscious.

What you know is power. Why? Because you are knowing the truth of all existence, knowing this truth *as* the very Mind that is God. Actually, what you are knowing *is that which you are.* Right here is where the power of this knowing lies.

> You cannot be anything that you are not conscious of being. You cannot have or experience anything that is unknown to you. In addition to this, you can never be conscious of anything that is unknown to God.

All that is manifest, all that is active in you or as you, all that appears as your experience, is known to the All-knowing Mind. This is the only Mind that exists and functions *as* your Mind now, this instant. Nothing forms itself outside of or apart from Mind. Nothing acts contrary to the uninterrupted activity of perfect Mind. No thing, condition, or experience is known to another mind.

Actually, God-Mind knows no conditions. The word *conditions* implies change; God is forever the changeless One. It also implies something opposite, something else from which a comparison may be drawn. There are no opposites, no conditions, no comparisons in the one infinite One, All.

Now for a brief recapitulation: God is the one and only Mind. God-Mind is omnipresent, omniactive, omnipotent and is forever in ceaseless operation. What God knows is all that is known. God-Mind can know nothing outside of or apart from Its infinite Self-containment. This Self is eternal, immutable, beginningless, endless perfection. This Mind, knowing Its own perfection, is individualized, identified right here and now as the Mind with which you are aware of your Self. This conscious Life, identified *as You,* is conscious of living, of being alive as your Life. This is the Mind that is writing these words, and this is the Mind that is reading them. The response you feel to what you are reading here is God-Mind recognizing and responding to Its own truth.

This is *you,* dear reader. Accept this truth; acknowledge it because it is your truth.

Chapter IV

FREEDOM

The people that walked in darkness have seen a great light: they that dwell in the land of the shadow of death, upon them hath the light shined ...

For thou hast broken the yoke of his burden, and the staff of his shoulder, the rod of his oppressor ...

For unto us a child is born, unto us a son is given: and the government shall be upon his shoulder: and his name shall be called Wonderful, Counseller, The mighty God, The everlasting Father, The Prince of Peace.

—Isa. 9: 2, 4, 6

Many and varied are the interpretations applied to the foregoing verses, the most widely accepted one being that it is a prophecy of the birth of Jesus. A deeper insight into the spiritual significance of this Scripture reveals that it is not a prophecy at all. *It is a revelation.* Here we find clearly stated the truth of existence *as it is,* as it has always been, and as it will always be.

You will note that these verses indicate an accomplished fact. For instance, the people *have seen* a great light, and upon them hath the light *shined.* Unto us a child *is born,* a son *is given,* and

45

the government *shall be* upon his shoulder. Who is the son? Who is to be self-governed? Upon whom hath the Light shined? You are the Son. You are the illumined One. How can this be? It is because you are just what God is, identified *as* you.

There can be no Son, no identity, other than God identified, individualized, and expressed *as* the Son. The Father and the Son are really *one*, and as one, they are eternally Self-governed. In this conscious Self-government, there are no laws, no limitations, no restrictions. Here, Principle is established, and God, Principle, does not violate Itself.

If we were to accept all the daily reports presented to us, we would feel that this is very far from being manifest in the world today. On all sides, we hear and read of the brutal oppression by dictatorships and the continual struggle for more power by the despots in this world of appearance. Probably the most sinister aspect of this power-mad struggle is the effort to gain control over the intelligence of that which we call man.

There are many laudable attempts being made today to combat this diabolic appearance of nonexistent evil. We have no quarrel with these attempts or with the organizations through which they are being made. We do realize this, how-ever — that there never has been an organization or a group of individuals that could solve the

46

problems of the world *on the level of the problem.* If that could have been done, it would have been done long ago. On the contrary, this spurious claim to power has appeared to increase and become more vicious.

About now, you may be questioning: "But is there nothing that we can do about this?" Indeed there is, and that is just why the Ultimate revelation is here. We make no effort to "handle it mentally," neither do we bury our heads in the sand, in self-deception. *We know what we know, and what we know is power, the only power.* Why? Because of ourselves we know nothing, can do nothing; but as the Mind which is God expressed, we know all and can do all.

Let us perceive just how to go about seeing through this monstrous claim of an evil power and presence. In this, as in every situation, we instantly and continuously know the allness, the omnipotence of God. There are not two minds, one evil and the other good. God is the *only* Mind, and there is no evil mind capable of planning or carrying out vicious plans. There is neither a person nor a personal mind with power to be evil or to do evil.

All the puny efforts of the misidentification called man are completely devoid of power and can have no influence or control over you or your affairs. And this is true of all of us, no matter how overwhelming the false evidence may be to the contrary. This unlimited vision will disclose the greatest dictator, the most cruel dictatorship, to be the farthest removed from actuality.

Throughout the ages, there have appeared dictators and dictatorships, but they have always come to nothing. Why? Because they were nothing to begin with. The more power evil *assumes* the less power it has because God, Good, is omnipotent. The more unprincipled it appears to be the less power it has to enforce its so-called laws because God is the only Principle. There is no intelligent evil and no evil intelligence. In fact, *there is no evil.*

There is no person, either good or bad. Therefore we know that the misidentification called man has no power to save or destroy either the nation or the world. God is His own power, and He is not Self-destructive. Neither is He aware of a need to be saved from evil. We are not too concerned when our particular candidate is not elected if we know that God, and God alone, is power and that God is wholly and entirely good.

The delusion that this man can be our savior or that man our destroyer plays a large part in the fantasy of world evil.

> "I will overturn, overturn, overturn, it: and it shall be no more, until he come whose right it is; and I will give it him" (Ezek 21:27).

What does this mean? Who is it who is to come into a realization of his divine nature? Who is it that is to perceive his only identity as the presence of the power of God and the power of the presence of God? It is God Himself, identified, expressed, and individualized as you, as me, as all.

There is basic truth underlying the fact that anything pretending to be the power to enslave, restrict, or limit always meets with our greatest resistance. Inherently we know that freedom is our natural state of being, and of course we insist on asserting that freedom. Our genuine and only identity knows that anything pretending to exert the power to restrict, limit, or destroy our freedom is only the false assumption of nonexistent evil. The consciousness of this eternal, unlimited freedom forever abides in our identity as God identified. As this identity, we *know* that we are free, unlimited, unrestricted, unregimented. We *know* that we are Self-governed because we are the very principle of our being and universe. We know that there is no such thing as a law of injustice and that we are the very expression of the principle of justice in full and complete operation. We know that there are no restrictive laws, that there is only Principle in unopposed control of Its own expressed Being.

There is no one existing who is devoid of an awareness of this truth. That is why there has always been, and will continue to be, such a great resistance to domination, restriction, regimentation. It is true that in the seeming world of man the resistance takes the form of a human struggle for freedom. This is because, in the illusion of a material world, there seems to be an acceptance of evil, and this acceptance includes the spurious claim that it has power to restrict, limit, and destroy. But when evil is seen to be *nothing*, the enlightened one perceives that there is no evil power, and thus, no one is under the influence or domination of its mythical claims to presence and power.

This is not a material world being threatened with destruction. We are not mortals with bodies of matter facing annihilation by atom or hydrogen bombs. God is Spirit and God is All. Spirit is the substance that comprises the universe, the world, and the entirety of you and all. What can destroy Spirit, God? What Mind exists that is conscious of a destructive element? What Mind exists that fears evil? Accepts it? Or believes in it? *None.* There is no such mind existing. There is no mind conceiving evil, no mind accepting evil, no mind affected by evil. There is no evil to be conceived or accepted that can affect in the least the one Mind which is God. And this God-Mind is the only Mind that is ever expressed or identified as the Mind of anyone.

As stated before, that which we know is power. What you and I and others of spiritual vision are perceiving is the *only* power that will reveal the utter futility, impotence, non-intelligence, and the nothingness of this bloated claim to an evil power. In the same way, omnipresent freedom is revealed where bondage, and even slavery, has seemed to be. There is no other way. Indeed, we can expose and dispose of these pretensions of nonexistent evil. We are the Light that reveals its nothingness. But let us not be lulled to sleep; let us not dawdle. Let us rather be about our Father's business, actively operating *as* the Light.

Always the spurious claims of evil pretend to be a power that can bind, limit, restrict, or destroy. Frequently they masquerade under the name of "law." We hear of the law of cause and effect, the law of age, the law of retribution, and countless other so-called laws. Who or what makes and enforces these laws? Who is the person that is helpless in the grip of such monstrous injustices? There is neither law nor a necessity for law where Principle is All. In spiritual perception, we know that there is no one "under the law" and no person subject to bondage, restriction, or destruction.

It makes no difference whether assumptive evil claims power as a dictatorship, a law of cause and effect, a law of age, or any other restrictive law—it is entirely devoid of either presence or power. It is just as devoid of existence or power when it pretends to be a law governing the body as it is when it claims to be a law governing the body politic.

In enlightenment, we know that we are, and have always been, free. We do not struggle to regain that which has never been lost. We never look to that which is called man for help in any way. We know that the misidentification called man has no more power for good than it has for evil. We do not declare the truth and deny the evil in the effort to become free. We know that we really do "live, and move, and have our being" in the kingdom of God and that the kingdom of God is here and now in us, *as* us—yes, as our entire Life, Being, body and experience.

We are not the misidentification called man. We are the Father identified as the Son, and never have we been other than we are at this instant. We also know that the truth which is true for us is also true for all.

> It is our clear perception that will reveal the truth of omnipresent freedom. We are the Light—let us show forth.

Chapter V

IDENTITY

There are two words in the English language that epitomize clearly and concisely *just what it is that constitutes you*. Therefore, it is of prime impor tance that a deep and thorough perception of the meaning of these words be established in and *as* your Consciousness. These words are *absolute* and *identity*. These two words, when combined, are a wonderful definition of *you*. Realizing this, you will wish to study carefully the follow ing definitions of them, as found in *Webster's Unabridged Dictionary*.

"Absolute: Free from imperfection, complete in its own character. Free from limits, restrictions or qualifications."

"Identity: Reality at its deepest level, in which subject and object are one."

Much has been written and said about the Absolute, and it has all been good. Yet until we perceive that all that is known of this Absolute is the truth of our own identity, It apparently does not fulfill Itself *as* us. *All that is true of the Absolute is true of each one of us.* Why? Because the Absolute is our identity. Yes, the Absolute, free from imperfection, restriction, or qualification, *is* identified as you and me and as *All*. Your identity is "reality at its deepest level, in which subject and object are one." And this *One* is *You*, the only You in existence.

This identity is not something you are striving to become. Rather it is what you genuinely are, what you have always been, and what you will ever continue to be. It makes no difference what problems may seem to be confronting you or how far from the realization of it you may appear to be — *this is the truth of you, and it is true this instant.*

Just about now, you may be asking, "But why don't I know it? Why am I not manifesting it?" Dear reader, you *do* know it; you *are* manifesting it. Only in the mistaken sense of your identity can inharmonies and difficulties appear. But this mistaken sense of identity is not yours. It just isn't you. It is neither your identity nor your Consciousness of Being. In fact, it is entirely spurious, having no mind to give it reality.

During the months when the author was seeking light on this word *identity*, an incident seemingly long-forgotten suddenly reappeared to memory with crystal clearness. Knowing that Mind is constantly fulfilling Itself as the omnipresent answer to every question, consciousness was kept open and receptive for the revelation concerning this reappearance. It was through the Light, revealing the significance of this occurrence, that the full and glorious truth of this word *identity* was perceived. It is for this reason that you are to receive the revelation.

This incident occurred long ago, when the author was a so-called teenage schoolgirl. A hypnotist came to the small town where she was living and attending school. As this was considered quite an event, her whole class attended the performance as a group.

There was one lad in the class who was exceedingly shy. So much so that it was most difficult for him to stand before the class when called upon for any reason. When the hypnotist asked for someone to come on stage for his demonstration, the other boys in the group literally catapulted that timid boy onto the stage.

As soon as the lad was seated, the hypnotist told him that he was fastened to the seat of the chair and that he couldn't possibly extricate himself. In spite of all his efforts to free himself, he was apparently incapable of standing until the hypnotist told him that he was free and could arise from that chair.

Next, he was assured that he had a large apple fastened to the end of his nose. His contortions in the attempt to remove that nonexistent apple were ridiculous and, to us, hilariously funny, especially to those of us who knew him well. When the boy was finally released, he was so embarrassed that he slunk from the stage, left the theater at once, and refused to attend school for several days.

This episode has been set forth in detail because it will be most helpful to you in receiving the Light that is to dawn on this word *identity*. What had happened to that lad? Had he changed? Had he become someone other than himself? No, not at all. What did appear to happen was this: he seemed to have *temporarily surrendered his identity*. Remember, though, it was only a seeming surrender and of short duration. Had he really surrendered his identity? Not at all. When he returned to school again, he was identically the same shy lad we had known before. Not one single thing had happened to his identity. Even when he was apparently in the throes of that experience, *he was the same identity*. So, you perceive, he had not surrendered his identity.

Here is the revelation:

> We, too, have seemed to temporarily surrender our identity. But it is only a seeming surrender. Actually, our identity has not been changed; neither has it been affected in any way. Throughout all of eternity, our individual identity has existed as it is at this very instant—*perfect, entire, and gloriously free.*

There *is* one Mind identifying Itself as each one of us, and this Mind is not subject to hypnosis or surrender. Indeed, there is no mind existing capable of usurping the one Mind that is *the All-Mind*. God, the only Mind, never surrenders His own Identity. God is infinite Identity and is infinitely identified. God is infinite individuality and is infinitely individualized. *God does not surrender or change Its individualized Identity revealed as You.*

The you that you are right now is the identical you that has always existed and will continue to exist forever. You are without beginning, change, or ending. Never have you been other than your self. Now when you say, "I and my Father are one," you will know that what you really mean is, "I and my Father are identical." God is the only *I* that can identify Itself as the *I* of you.

There is no becoming. God never became your identity. You are as old as God because *your identity has always been included in the allness of God as your identity.* Was this *I* ever born? Can this *I* ever come to an end? Does this *I* ever surrender Its Identity? Does God surrender Himself?

Reader, do you realize that you are necessary to the completeness of God? If you were to lose your identity, God would at that instant be incomplete. Why? Because you, your identity, has always been included in the allness of God. If there was ever a time when you began, there was also a time when God came into being. If that could be true, God would not be eternal. Actually, there would have been a time when there was no God.

Let us return for a moment to that word *misidentification.* Thoughtful contemplation of this word reveals that *mis*identification is *non*identification. The false identity we have *appeared* to assume is nonidentity. It is entirely a spurious assumption of an individual, a life, a being, and a body that is nonexistent. This does not mean, however, that you, your life, your being, and your body are without existence. Neither does it mean that your individual identity is something nebulous, intangible, separate from practical everyday living.

What, then, *is* this mistaken sense of identity? How did it begin? When did it start? And what caused it? These are questions that must be answered if you are to have the complete revelation on this.

This entire mistaken sense of being stems from one word: *creation.* Creation implies beginning. Anything that has beginning is subject to change, and it must also have an ending.

> God is not a creator. Thus, there is no creation as it has appeared in this mistaken sense of identity.

Throughout the ages, the nations of the world have each had their own myths about the Creator and the creation of the world and man. In the western world, the record of creation as given in Genesis, chapters one and two of the Bible, have been generally accepted as authentic. No one questions the authenticity of much that is found in our beloved Bible. But the story of creation as set forth there is a *myth*.

If we accept that myth of creation as true, if we believe that Adam and Eve were created, had a beginning, we are going to have to accept everything that follows, *including an ending*—not only for Adam and Eve, but for you, for me, and for all of us. Do you doubt this? If so, read the genealogical record of the descendants of Adam as given in both the Old and the New Testaments.

This mythological concept of existence is not confined exclusively to our Bible. Every religion has its own Bible, and within each of these Bibles you will find some mythical explanation of the so-called beginning of the universe and man.

Of course, this is all in the realm of fantasy; but just so long as we accept it, identify ourselves with it, we will appear to be included in its fallacies. This is *misidentification*. Always remember:

> You, your identity, is entirely unaffected by and unconcerned with this fantasy.

It is most necessary to keep this in mind if you are to understand the following paragraph.

In the interim of seeming misidentification, we do appear to manifest and experience that with which we identify ourselves. Have you ever noticed that many doctors who are specialists in heart trouble succumb to that ailment? Frequently the specialist in malignant growths becomes afflicted with the very condition he is specializing in eradicating.

The author once knew of a young man who had been terrified for years by a fear of bees. What happened? In a locality where bees were virtually unknown, he was fatally stung by a bee. Please understand very clearly here that none of these things actually took place. Why, though, did they *appear* to happen? *Because that with which these individuals identified themselves seemed to become manifest in their experience.*

Of course, the only purpose in setting forth the false pictures in the foregoing paragraph is to draw an analogy for you. All of this will become more and more clear to you as you continue in your study of this book.

As stated before, there was never an Adam created. Therefore, Adam and all his so-called descendants are nonexistent. If we identify ourselves with the race of Adam, the nonexistent, we are seemingly sentencing ourselves to non-existence, death.

In what way do we seem to do this? First, we seem to do so by yielding to the assumption that we were created; that we were born as humans, as mortals; that we came forth from human parentage. Next, we seem to do so by accepting the false evidence of the universe, the world, the body as material, with beginning, change, and ending. Last, but equally important, we seem to do so by the seeming surrender of our mind, consciousness, to an imposition of the fantasy that there is a mind, a consciousness, identified as us, that is other than God. Bear in mind, though, that your genuine and *only* identity is completely untouched by all of this illusion. Even the word *illusion* gives a false impression because before there can be an illusion, there must be a person capable of suffering under that illusion. The truth is: *no such person exists.*

You may have noticed throughout this book that frequently the words *You* and *Yours* are cap-italized. Why? Because You are not a human being or a mortal being at all. Rather, You are a divine Being. You are God being You. Your Life is God-Life identified *as* your Life; Your Mind, Consciousness, is God-Mind, God-Consciousness identified *as* your Mind—yes, as your conscious awareness of your entire Being, activity, body, and experience.

Of yourself, you have no power or presence that can either identify or misidentify itself. You do not identify yourself as God. On the contrary, it is always God who identifies Himself *as* You. It is never through a struggle that this is realized. It is in the great peace of quiet acceptance of God, and God alone—as *all* there is to you, *all* there is of your Life, Mind, Being, and Body—that the glorious Truth reveals Itself. It is when you can say, "I thank you, Father; I know that I am just what You are *as me,"* that all false sense of identity is obliterated and that the *I* that is God is known to be the identity that is your *I.*

Yes, God is the only Life, Mind, Being, and Body. God is not only perfect—*He is the Perfection of the Perfect.* God is infinite, All-inclusive. Within His infinitude is contained all individuality, all identity. There is distinction of identity, but it is ever the same God, identifying Itself, individualizing Itself, presenting Itself as each individual identity.

God, being eternal Life, Mind, Being, and Body, cannot possibly identify Himself as a temporal life, mind, being, or body. God, being without beginning, change, or ending, cannot individualize Himself as a being with birth, change, or death. God, being forever existent, cannot identify Himself as an individual who is born into existence and dies out of existence. God, being infinite, eternal Perfection, cannot individualize Himself as imperfection. Forever immutable, He can only identify Himself as Immutability. God, Mind, forever conscious of His eternal, changeless, perfect existence, can never identify Himself *as a mind that is unconscious of this same perfect existence.* In fact, only that which God *is* can He identify Himself *as.*

Could God, being All-inclusive, knowing Himself to *be All,* possibly identify Himself as a consciousness of lack, limitation, or poverty? Can you be conscious of something that is unknown to God? With what mind can you know anything that is unknown to God-Mind? What presence or power can present itself to you that is not God-known, God-individualized? What Mind *exists* that could know anything that was unknown to God-Mind? What Mind exists that does *not* know Itself as God individualized, God identified? There is power in the realization of the answer to that last question.

The mistaken sense of identity may assume many forms. Sometimes it appears as an inability of the body to act normally, as hypnosis reacted on the boy who seemed unable to get up from the chair. Again, it may appear as something added to the body, as the nonexistent apple seemed real on the end of the boy's nose. It may appear as a mind capable of injustice, dishonesty, or cruelty. Limitation, restriction, avarice, greed are other aspects it may assume. It is impossible to mention the many guises under which the mistaken sense of identity may appear. It makes no difference how it appears, it has only one name. That name is *nothing*. God is the only *Something* in existence, and God can only appear, individualize, manifest, as the Perfection which He is.

If evil could exist and identify itself as you, it would have to exist in and as God. If this were true, it would be eternal, changeless, and forever an element of your Being. It would also exist as an established fact of each individual identity. If this could be true, God would have to be the One including the evil and also the one experiencing it. Ridiculous, isn't it? Yet it would all be true if evil could exist and be identified as you or your experience. Surely you can see now that if it were possible for evil to be, it would have to be the Mind which is God, for it would be included *in* and *as* His Consciousness. If God were aware of it, no one could hope to escape being conscious of it.

All that exists is known to the Mind that is God. Evil is not included in this Consciousness; therefore, there is no consciousness of evil. Being nonexistent, it is nothing. Can nothing make itself into something? Can non-intelligence, ignorance, express itself as Intelligence capable of identifying Itself? Can nothing, non-existence, give itself form, substance, activity, and intelligence? Can nothing identify itself as something? Where does evil get the intelligence with which it can claim identity, function as identity, or manifest as identity?

Any attempt to identify evil as something having form, substance, activity, mind, or power is an attempt to make something out of nothing. It is fruitless, futile, and impossible.

All of our seeking and searching for the Truth has been simply the one Identity which we are, insisting upon manifesting Itself.

We may have thought that we were the seeker. We may have even taken some credit for our dedication to the search. Actually, we did not choose this Truth. We had no choice. "Ye have not chosen me, but I have chosen you" (John 15:16). The You that You are *insists* on being You, your only Identity. "They shall all know me, from the least of them unto the greatest" (Jer. 3:34). Who is this "me" referred to in the foregoing quotation? It is You; it is God identified as your Life, Mind, Being, And Body. Bible quotations take on a new and glorious significance when spiritually discerned.

Dear reader, are you now asking if there is anything you can do that will enable you to perceive more clearly the *I* that you are? Yes, there is, and you are doing it right now. The inner response you feel to what you have been reading here is You *responding to Yourself.* It is the Self being conscious of Its identity. It is God-Consciousness identifying Itself *as* your Consciousness.

Of course, this does not mean that you are changing or exchanging one identity for another. How could you? You have never been any other than the one eternal Self you are in this instant. It is never a putting off, or getting rid of, a false identity. Rather it is a *seeing through* a mistaken concept of identity enabling the You that you *are* to emerge. This is Self-identification, Self-expression.

Much is being heard these days about self-expression. Most of it has nothing to do with expressing the Self that you are. You don't express this Self; It expresses Itself *as* you. There is a vast difference between this Self-expression and self-expression as it is generally accepted. In fact, most self-expression is selfish expression. It appears as a little self attempting to do something, to be something of itself. It appears as a false sense of ambition, a desire for self-glorification, a spreading of itself as though it were *something of itself.*

All this appears to be going on in the misidentification. However, you will not be caught in that net. You know too much. You know what Jesus meant when he said, "Of mine own self I can do nothing" (John 5:30). But you also know what he meant when he said, "the Father that dwelleth in me, he doeth the works" (John 14:10).

Yes, God, identified as Jesus, performed the works. And God, identified as you and me, is performing His own works today. What are these *works* that are being performed? They are God's perfect omnipresence, omniaction and omnipotence manifested as the actuality of all that exists. God's perfect substance is being manifested as the substance of all form. The beauty that is God is being manifested *as* the beauty of all form and substance. God, as perfect Omniaction, is being revealed *as* the activity of each identity. God, Omnipotence, is being known to be the only

Power that is present or in operation. Omni-present Perfection is being manifested, identified, as the only Presence of the one who appears to be in need of help or healing. These are the works that are being performed today as they were when Jesus walked and worked beside the Galilean Sea.

What is our part in all this? It is to accept, to acknowledge God as all that can be identified as us. It is to claim our identity as God, revealing, individualizing, manifesting, and identifying Him-self *as* the entirety of our Life, Mind, Body, Being, and all our activity.

Refusing to acknowledge, accept, or claim a false—even nonexistent—identity, we find that it has no presence or power to make any claims upon us. Refusing to identify ourselves with anything but God, we discover with joy that nothing but God is identified as us. Refusing to honor or give credence to *anything* other than God, we perceive that *nothing* but God has existence *as* us or anything concerning us.

No matter what nametag may have been applied to the misidentification of you, whether Mary, John, or whatever, you have but one name, and that name is I AM. This is the name in which the works are performed. It is the name you have always had and will ever continue to have. Truly, "the gift of God" is Himself, His Life identified as your Life, His Mind identified as your Mind,

His omnipotent Omnipresence identified as your Power and as your *only* Presence.

This is *you*. This is your identity as revealed in the definition of the Absolute. Accept It—*be It*—for It is your Self.

Chapter VI

BODY

Glorify God in your body,
and in your spirit, which are God's.
—*1 Cor. 6:20*

As we pursue the study of Truth, searching through ancient as well as modern writings, one salient fact becomes more and more apparent. Almost nothing that is tangible, understandable, has been written about the body. One wonders why this should be true when so many of the seeming ills presenting themselves have to do with the body.

In the most ancient spiritual records, one finds a marked tendency to revile the body. It has been said that Plotinus actually seemed ashamed of having a body. This tendency to malign the body has continued throughout the centuries and has even crept into some of our present-day metaphysical literature. One form it assumes is the denial of the body; another form is in ignoring the body.

All of this is based on a false premise of what it is that constitutes the body; and a false premise can only lead to a false conclusion. Just so long as we revile the body we will *appear* to have a vile

69

body that can suffer, weaken, and die. It is only when we perceive the genuine nature of body that we can "glorify God in the body" as well as in Spirit; Soul, Life, and Mind. No so-called human mind can reveal to us this Body, but the spiritual perception culminating in the revelation of this Body of Light is an ever-present possibility with all of us.

It is a mistake to deny the body, and to attempt to ignore it is futile. Who can completely ignore his body? Don't we feed it, clothe it, bathe it, and move it about? Of course we do, and these are normal everyday activities. There is nothing wrong about acknowledging the existence of the body. The only thing wrong has been in the *kind* of body we have been acknowledging. The misconception has been in interpreting the nature of the body with which we have been identifying ourselves.

Why is it that we have understood so little about the nature of body? Because it is the most difficult to comprehend and requires the ultimate in spiritual perception. Yet this final illumination is, beyond a doubt, the greatest requisite to complete Self-recognition. Why? Because it is the misconception, the misidentification of body, which is the greatest contributing factor to our false sense of being separate from God.

It is not too difficult for most of us to perceive that God is the one and only Life and that this same God-Life is identified as the Life of each one of us. Likewise, the fact that God is the one indivisible Mind, individualized as the Mind of each identity, is quickly seen and understood. Spirit, Soul, Truth, and Love as inseparable; yet, individualized, can readily be perceived. This is because *the indivisible essence of Life, Mind, Spirit, Soul, Truth, Love is not perceptible to the so-called material senses.* However, the body does *appear* to be recognizable to these deceptive senses.

All misidentification of the body is due to the seeming surrender of our genuine identity to these spurious senses.

Dozens of examples can be, and have been, set forth citing the unreliability of the testimony of these false senses. That is all good, but it isn't enough. We must see farther than that if we are to have the ultimate revelation of body. Of what avail is it to us to know that the testimony of the so-called material senses is false, if we still acknowledge an identity capable of being victim-ized by this false testimony?

> In fact, we are to realize that there are no material senses, there are no mortals bearing witness to any false testimony, and there is no man or mind that can recognize or experience the result of these nonexistent senses.

In order to see clearly just what body *is*, let us expose and dispose of that which body *is not*. Let us face this thing squarely and see what this mind *that is no mind* claims to report to us about body.

According to this non-mind, the body is supposed to be temporal, to have beginning, change, and ending. It is supposed to have been created and to be the projection of other temporal bodies. In turn, it is supposed to create more temporal bodies. It is supposed to be born, to live, to suffer and enjoy, to sicken and weaken, and finally to die. It is supposed to be composed of material elements constantly in a state of change; and finally, these material elements are supposed to decompose.

It is supposed to be something that can live of itself and can die of itself. Each individual body is supposed to have its own substance, form, activity, and life span separate and apart from the one indivisible Life. Each individual body is supposed to have its own mind, its own intelligence, separate and apart from the one inseparable Mind. The life of each individual body is supposed to begin a few months before birth and to end at death. Each individual body is supposed to occupy a certain amount of space for a certain length of time.

All of this is a myth, a supposition; there is no truth in it. The assumption that the body is temporal, that it comes into existence and goes out of existence, is entirely false.

All the religions based upon the Bible teach that there is at least a possibility of life after death. Most of the Eastern religions teach that the individual soul existed before birth and continues after death. However, all of them accept the myth that the body begins and ends. If the promise of the Bible, "There shall be no more death," is ever to be fulfilled, *we must begin now* to perceive that the Body is as eternal, as indestructible, as the Soul.

Let us return to the Bible quotation given at the beginning of this chapter: "Glorify God in your body, and in your spirit, which are God's" (1 Cor. 6:20). The truth about body is clearly set forth in this quotation. It has been right there in the Bible, and we have read it again and again; yet the spiritual meaning of this all-important passage has eluded us.

What is the spiritual significance of this quotation? Here it is plainly stated that *God is the only Body and God is the only Soul, Spirit.* Here it is stated that you are to glorify God in *your* body; but it also states that your body and spirit are God's Body and God's Spirit. How can this be accepted when the evidence opposing it is almost overwhelming? It cannot be, and will not be, accepted by the assumptive human mind. Nonetheless, the fact remains that this is a true statement of body.

Soul, Spirit, and Body are not different elements. They are one, and that One is God. Soul and Body do not fuse at birth and separate at death. Rather they are eternally one, and as one, they are indivisible. God is Soul and Body, and God is never separated into partials.

In the Ultimate, we see farther than that. We perceive that Life, Mind, Substance, Being, Soul, and Body are God and are embodied as the body of God. God comprises the All of His own infinite embodiment. There is no unexpressed God; and God, as Body, is expressed, individualized, identified as the body of you, of me, and of all things.

If this were not true, God would not be All as all. If this were not true, there would have to be God *and something existing that was not God*. To speak of God *and* the body is like saying that God is All but that there is something else besides that Allness. If we are to accept God as All, *we must acknowledge God to be All—as the Body as well as the Mind, the Spirit and the Soul.*

Dear reader: do you accept this? Do you believe it? Either this revelation strikes an answering chord in you, or it does not. There is no middle way; there is no qualification. Neither can there be a partial acceptance of this. This is important because it is impossible to perceive the Ultimate Absolute without a full acknowledgment that the Allness of God includes the Body as well as the Mind, Spirit, Life, and the Soul.

Here you are on holy ground. Here you stand alone. No one can perceive this truth for you; no one can even help you to see it. If it is impossible for you to accept this fully, it is better for you to put this book aside for the time being; for the complete revelation which is to follow is based entirely upon this truth. If you can fully accept it, regardless of all the seeming evidence to the contrary, you are indeed at the threshold of illumination. Blessed be your eyes, for they see, and seeing, understand. "The light of the body is the eye: if therefore thine eye be single, thy whole body shall be full of light" (Matt. 6:22).

Let us now continue in this revelation of the Body of Light. It is clear now that the universe and all it contains is God. Nothing has existence outside of God because there is no outside to the All. God comprises the entirety of His allness. The very allness, the infinity of God, is the body of God.

"There is one body, and one Spirit" (Ephes. 4:4). Yes, there is one body—the body of God. As stated before, there is no unexpressed God. Indeed, God fulfills Himself as His expression of His own Being. God can only express Himself as that which He is. Just as you are individually you, although you are God identified as you, so *your body is individually your body, although it is God's body individualized as your body.*

You can now understand that in order to know what comprises the body, it is essential to perceive what God is as the body. Before we continue, though, let this point be clear: we are not speaking of a body that is intangible, floating around in mid-air. Neither are we referring to a body of matter. But we are alluding to the body that we use every day, for this is the body we have been misidentifying as matter, as temporal, changing, aging, and dying. This is the body that is "the temple of the living God."

What is God, identified as the body? Well, to make a beginning, God is Life. Is there more than one God, one Life; or is God-Life the only Life that lives? The answer to that is obvious.

> God is the only Life that lives and is identified as your Life this instant. Your body is alive; it lives. What Life could be alive, what Life could live as the Life of your body, other than God-Life?

This Life is indivisible. Never is It separated or divided into countless little lives. But It is expressed, identified, manifest as your individual Life and the Life of your individual body. For instance, one might say that the life of the finger was distinctly the life of the finger; but still it would be inseparable from the life of the entire body. In this way we can perceive that while our life is distinctly the life of this body, still it is inseparable from the entirety of the one infinite Life eternally embodied as one infinite Body.

God, Life, is eternal, beginningless, changeless, endless. Can eternal Life be also a temporal life? Can eternal Life ever be, or become, a temporal life to Its own entirety, to Its own embodiment?

Life is not an attribute of God. *Life is God.*

Did Life, God, ever come into being, and can It ever go out of being? Did Life ever enter Its own embodiment, and can It depart from that embodiment? Is Life something other than Its embodiment, or is It the very embodiment of Itself? *Does It inhabit the body, or is It embodied as the body?*

The answers to these questions are inherent in and as your consciousness; thus, you already know them. However, at this point, it is well to contemplate anew these questions and the answers to them. This quiet contemplation will open your consciousness for the revelation which is to appear.

Now you are aware that the Life that is God is embodied as His own entirety or embodiment and that this Life is beginningless, changeless, endless, *as the Life that lives as Its own embodiment.* As God is and has ever been complete, all the Life that is individualized at this instant has always existed as God-Life. Your identical Life has forever been included in and *as* this Life individualized. Body is not excluded from this Life individualized as your Life.

Actually, eternal Life is expressed, manifested, embodied as your eternal Body. Just

77

as the Life that is God does not inhabit His embodiment but lives as that embodiment, so it is that this Life, individualized as the Life of your body, does not inhabit the body but lives as the Life of your body. There is no such thing as eternal Life inhabiting a temporal body. Rather it is that the body is as eternal as the Life that lives, sustains, and maintains Itself as Its own eternal embodiment.

Life is manifest as activity. You know, of course, that death is pronounced when all *apparent* activity of the misidentification of body has come to an end. But Life does not come to an end.

Life, Activity, is God; and God-activity is without birth or death, without beginning or ending. And this is the Life that lives, the Activity that is active, embodied as your individual body.

Of course, Life individualized as the body does not exclude Soul, Mind, Spirit, Consciousness. Never can God be divided into elements. He is one infinite, all-inclusive whole. Life, Spirit, Soul, Mind, Essence, Being, and Body are One and, as One, are neither separate nor separable.

For instance, there is no mindless Life, no lifeless Mind. Life is intelligence and Mind is ceaselessly active. Nothing can stop or interfere with Its activity. It is known now that the mind remains active even in sleep. Have you ever gone to sleep with some seeming problem uppermost in thought and awakened with the consciousness of the solution to that problem? This has taken place quite frequently with the author, and no doubt you have had the same experience. This is just one example of the eternal oneness of Mind and Life, Activity.

There is no soulless Life or Mind, and there is no lifeless, non-intelligent Soul. God is one integral whole which cannot be expressed as separate qualities or elements. Wherever God is expressed, He is expressed in His entirety.

It is exceedingly important that we understand this. Why? Because so much of our difficulty in knowing the nature of body has been due to dualism. We have been taught that Life, Soul, Mind were all qualities or elements inhabiting the body but that the body was composed of other elements of a material nature. Just so long as this mistaken theory is accepted, we will continue to have the *appearance* of death because it is the body that is supposed to live and the body that is supposed to die. This suppositional death will no longer appear when we are completely aware that Life, Mind, Soul, and Body are all one integral whole, not separated or separable into elements or qualities.

What is Soul as the body? As in all else, we return to the allness, the onliness of God. God is Soul, and the Soul that is God must be expressed. It *is* expressed; It *is* identified, individualized as the Soul of you, of me, and of all. Earlier in this chapter, we referred to the so-called material senses and that there is no man being victimized by these suppositional senses. It is imperative that we understand that there are no material senses and that there is no man being victimized by these suppositional senses. Just to say that these senses are false and that their testimony is unreliable isn't enough. We must go all the way and see *how* it is and *why* it is that there are no material senses and that there is no man having or experiencing these nonexistent senses.

Instead of five material senses, there is one Sense. This Sense is Soul, and Soul and Spirit are identical. Thus, the only Sense in existence must necessarily be Soul-Sense, spiritual Sense. This spiritual Sense is perception, awareness, Consciousness. It is this Soul-Sense that is constantly aware of Truth, reality, fact. It is Consciousness being conscious; Awareness being aware; Perception perceiving that which has existence. In the complete illumination of this, you will discover that *there is no division between the conscious perception and that which is perceived.* God is conscious Perception; but God is also the Substance of all that He perceives.

Now let us see how, and in what way, all of this pertains to body. You will need to follow very carefully that which is now about to be revealed. Step by step we have been leading up to this revelation: Soul, Life, Mind, Spirit, Principle is that which constitutes the body—and this is your body, the body you have always had and will always continue to have. This idea may seem startling to you or even confusing just now. It will become crystal clear, however, during the course of your study of this chapter.

God is Consciousness, and God-Consciousness is all that is identified *as* your Consciousness. God is conscious of Himself as You. God is conscious of Himself as your consciousness of your Self. *Your consciousness of your Self includes your body, just as God's consciousness of Himself includes His infinite embodiment.* Remember, though, that God comprises the entirety of His infinite embodiment as well as being the Consciousness of His embodiment.

In fact, His consciousness of His embodiment and His embodiment are the same thing. God-Consciousness identified as You includes His consciousness of body. This consciousness of body is identified as your consciousness of your body. Just as God-Consciousness is the very essence of His very embodiment, so your Consciousness is the essence, substance, of your embodiment. The point at which we are arriving is this:

> Your body is your Consciousness, your Soul, embodied. Your Consciousness is eternal God; and your Consciousness embodied is the body you have at this very instant. It never began, and it never began as your body. It can never end, and it can never end as your body.

Now can you see why we say that there is no creator and no creation? All that exists now has always existed and will forever exist. And this existence includes your body.

Yes, there is one Sense, and that is Soul-Sense. Your body is this spiritual Consciousness embodied. Only that which is included in and as the Mind, the Consciousness that is God, can be embodied as your body. Furthermore, the only Consciousness of embodiment is the Essence of that very embodiment.

Right about now is the time when you should begin to ask your Self some questions, knowing that the answers are inherent within this Self. Let the questions be something like this: as eternal Life embodied, do I have a body that had beginning? Do I have a body that is temporal? That was born? That must change, age, and die? If I believe that I was born as a human being with a material body, what was I before birth? Was I bodiless, intangible, without form? If I believe that the body must end in death, what will I be after death takes place? Will I be without form or substance?

If Consciousness is all that is ever embodied as my body, is my body not as eternal as is Consciousness? If eternal Life is embodied as my body, is not my body as eternal as the Life that is embodied? If I am eternal Consciousness, Mind, can I know anything about a beginning, a birth? Can I know anything about an ending, a death?

Can I know or have a body that was born or a body that can die? If I believe that I have a body that was born, how can I escape the belief that I have a body that must die? Doesn't anything that has a beginning necessarily have an ending?

Yes, these, and many more questions, will you ask of your Self. It is in the answers to these questions that full revelation appears.

For years there has been much belief in and speculation about reincarnation. We will not argue the merit or demerit of this belief. It is sufficient to realize this: the entire appearance of a material body, whether it be young, middle-aged, or old, is the product of the misidentification, the seeming surrender of our identity. It is possible, of course, that if this identity seemed to be surrendered once, it could again appear to be surrendered. But the fact remains that the misidentity is no identity; and our genuine and only Identity is never surrendered.

In addition to this, although the misidentity may seem to begin with birth and end at death, the *I* that you are and the *I* that I am can instantaneously and gloriously reveal Itself. This infinite *I*, individualized as you and manifest as your body, remains forever the same.

As Soul, Consciousness, are you confined, limited to the body? No! Never can you be limited or restricted. You are infinite as well as eternal. It is simply that you include your body in the

83

infinitude of your Consciousness. As the embodiment of Soul, Consciousness, what could you know *as* the body that is unknown to God, Mind? Can this conscious Perfection know or report imperfection, pain, disease, or abnormally as your body? Can conscious Life fear or know death? Can conscious Life, embodied, ever be threatened with an ending when Its very nature is eternality? Can conscious Perfection be or become conscious imperfection?

Dwell on these questions. Don't try to answer them; rather let the answers appear as the Light reveals your Self, including your eternal changeless Body.

Years ago, one with great spiritual insight said this to the author: "You are just what God knows about Himself." That tremendous statement of Truth was little understood at the time; but somehow it remained almost constantly in consciousness. So much so that it became a necessity to understand the spiritual significance of those words. The search has been long, but the revelation is glorious. However, it has come mainly from just such Self-questioning as that presented in this chapter. So continue with your Self-questioning. The answers are all within your Self, and they will be revealed. Have no fear, for they will be revealed in time. Even while you are questioning, remember that you are the very Consciousness in which the answers have always been contained.

Above all, never attempt to bring forth the answers through so-called human reasoning. The Truth is God; and the only Mind that can reveal It is the Mind that knows Itself to be Its own Truth. This is your Mind, and it is forever Self- revealing.

The Master well knew the exact nature of eternal, indestructible Consciousness embodied *as* his body. It was this that enabled Him to present his body instantly wherever he wished it to appear. It was this that enabled him to appear instantaneously in the room where the windows and doors were all closed, to disappear at will, and to walk on the water. He also knew that it was of the greatest importance that all of us partake of his consciousness of the nature of body. The following little understood passages from the Bible reveal this most emphatically:

> I am the living bread which came down from heaven: if any man eat of this bread, he shall live forever: and the bread that I will give is my flesh, which I will give for the life of the world ... Verily, verily, I say unto you, Except ye eat the flesh of the Son of man, and drink his blood, ye have no life in you. Whoso eateth my flesh, and drinketh my blood, hath eternal life ... He that eateth my flesh, and drinketh my blood, dwelleth in me, and I in him (John 6:51, 53,-54, 56).

These verses from the Bible are offensive to many. In fact, for years they were so to the author. But oh! — the glory of the Light that dawned when the true meaning of these verses was revealed. Here Jesus says plainly just what is necessary in order that even the *appearance* of death be overcome. Here he makes it clear that we must partake, that we must share in the awareness of just what body is before we can know that *eternal Body*, without beginning, change, or ending.

It is true that he referred to his body as flesh and blood. This was because that was all those about him were able to understand at the time. But he knew that his body was the temple of the living God, the indestructible abiding place of Life eternal. He was affirming that body is the very Christ-Consciousness embodied and that to partake of this Christ-Consciousness of body is to realize eternal Life.

> And after six days Jesus taketh Peter, James, and John his brother, and bringeth them up into an high mountain apart, And was transfigured before them: and his face did shine as the sun, and his raiment was white as the light. And, behold, there appeared unto them Moses and Elias talking with him (Matthew 17:1-3).

These inspiring verses give us an inkling of the Body of Light. Jesus did not put off one body and put on another. Rather it was that the eyes of the disciples were opened, and they were enabled to see him as he was and had been all the time.

Never make the mistake of attempting to visualize this body. It just can't be done, and the attempt can only lead to confusion. It is in the great silent peace of utter absorption in God-Consciousness that the illumination of body is revealed. This is *seeing* the Light by *being* the Light, perceiving the Light by the Light that is within you. There are no words with which to describe this glorious experience. But one thing can be said with certainty: when this takes place and your eyes are opened, you are fully aware that you, including your body, have always existed and will forever continue to exist.

In this Consciousness you know that there is no death and no material body that is subject to death.

What can you do to bring this about? Nothing of yourself. Certain it is that any effort along this line is futile. But it does come when you least expect it—sometimes suddenly, sometimes gradually; sometimes in one way and sometimes in another—*but it does come*. Yes, it sometimes comes in a moment of great need, when the heart cries out, "Father, of myself I am nothing, have nothing, know nothing. Give me light." It may come when you are deep in meditation, communing with the God who is the entirety of your Being. No one can say when or how it may appear. The author knows one woman who had her first illumination while seeing the sun rise over the Grand Canyon. Needless to say, months of consecrated study and meditation had preceded this revelation.

What has all this to do with body? It is through the dawning of this Light that the full glory of the imperishable Body is revealed. But no one has to wait for this event before knowing the truth about body.

You can begin right now, this very instant, to perceive and claim your genuine and only identity as the very presence and power of God individualized *as* you, your Mind, Consciousness, Soul, and Body. If you will do this, and persist in the face of every spurious appearance to the contrary, you will discover the true meaning of the statement, "I and my Father are one."

Chapter VII

BEAUTY

What is beauty? Why are we attracted to beauty, and repelled by its opposite? Beauty is natural; beauty, just as health, is normal. In fact, *Beauty is God.* Therefore Beauty is Life, Mind, Soul, and all that God *is.* God is infinite Beauty and infinitely beautiful. As God, Beauty is eternal, immutable, and eternally, infinitely expressed, individualized, identified.

A few years ago there was a program entitled, "Life Can Be Beautiful." The author has always thought that was a good title for a program. But we see farther than that. We know that Life *is* beautiful because Life is God, and God is Beauty.

Again, there is no unexpressed God. As Beauty, God is constantly expressing Itself, individualizing Itself, identifying Itself. Just as naturally as the flower or the leaf turns to the Light, so do we respond to the Beauty that is God.

Where is this Beauty that brings such joyous response? Is It something outside of you? Something desirable that must be attained? No! Is It temporal, fleeting, mutable? No! *Is It personal?* No! Beauty is as omnipresent, as immutable, as eternal as is God, for God *is* Beauty.

The Beauty that is God expresses Itself in countless ways and in infinite variety. It may appear as a sunset, a sunrise, the morning dew upon the grass, or the joyous song of a bird. It may appear as a beautiful scene or the beauty of some loved one. So often It appears when the face of someone who has suddenly seen the Light becomes radiant with joy. No matter in what way It appears, It is still God appearing, God expressing, God individualizing Itself as Beauty.

The musician, the composer, interprets this infinite beauty in terms of sound, harmony, rhythm, form, and color. Yes, music has form and color. Ask any composer; he will assure you that this is true. But art also has harmony, rhythm, form, and color. The artist interprets beauty as all these upon the canvas. But *it is the same indivisible, inseparable Beauty no matter how it may appear or be interpreted.* The nature lover is very apt to tell you that he feels closer to God when surrounded by the beauties of nature than at any other time. The integration of the beauty of the arts—music, painting, poetry, literature, sculpture, and many others—gives us an inkling of the indivisible nature of Beauty as God.

There is *no one* so depraved that he does not respond to Beauty in some form of expression.

The beauty of art, music, nature, or whatever, is One; but it appears as distinct facets of that same One. Where is all this enduring, imperishable beauty? *It is in you, in me, and in all of us.*

More than that, it is expressed *as* all of us. Beauty is as essential to completeness as is Life. We couldn't escape it, even if we wished and tried to escape. It is inherent in and *as* your very nature.

Let us take music, for example. (The author is a composer, and music is a natural medium of expression for her). Where is the music? Where is the harmony, color, form, and rhythm? Is it outside of the composer? No. Does he create it? No. On the contrary, it has forever been established *as it is.*

The composer knows that he creates nothing. *But he does listen.* Not a note is written until the tone is heard. No combination of notes is ever put on paper until the composer has heard those melodies or harmonies. Is he responsible for bringing it forth? No! The beauty of that music is God, and *God insists on expressing Himself as that beauty.*

Beauty is perfection. Have you ever noticed that the most perfect music, literature, and art endure and continue to bring joy to those who respond to such expression? This gives us a hint of the eternal, indestructible nature of the beauty of Perfection.

Have you not thrilled at hearing or beholding beauty in one form or another? Of course you have. What was it in you that responded to that beauty? Was it you as a person responding to something outside? No! Your response to beauty is God. God *as* you, recognizing, responding, and exulting in His own Being. In other words, God *as* you is the beauty, the expression of the beauty, and the response to the beauty.

In the case of the composer, it is God individualized *as* the beauty of the music, the expression of it, and as the composer who hears it and responds to it. The beauty that is God, the beauty of Perfection, expresses itself. We, as persons, do not express it. In fact, we, as persons, do not even exist. So how could we express beauty?

Never be mistaken about this: it is always *God* individualized, identified *as* you, but *never* you who is individualized as God. Only God is God, and only God individualizes Himself. *We must be clear on this.*

It has been said that beauty is fleeting and transitory. How can this be if God is beauty (and He is), if God is eternal, without beginning, change, or ending? Beauty does not change or come to an end. Neither does it have beginning. In order to exist, to have being, beauty must be eternal, immutable, imperishable, and indestructible.

What has this to do with you? *You are that Beauty expressed, individualized, identified.* The

Beauty that is God identified as you never began, and it never began *as* you. Neither can It change, fade, or disappear. Always remember that this Beauty that is expressed *as* you is the beauty of Perfection. You are not responsible for it either. God *is* His own expression of Himself; and He it is who maintains, sustains, and perpetuates Himself as all there is of you. This, of course, includes the Life, Mind, Soul, and Body which are eternal Beauty evidenced.

Yes, Life not only *can* be beautiful, Life *is* beautiful. And you are this beauty, identified not only as body but as the entirety of your being and experience. There is nothing ugly or sordid that can possibly be, or become, any part of your Life, Mind, Body, or experience. Why? Because God is the entirety of all of this, and God is eternally and infinitely All.

You see, whatever it is that has existence, whatever it is that appears before you, it is God existing and appearing *as that.* Whether it appears as an embodiment, an experience, an activity, or whatever, *it is still God, and God only,* evidencing, identifying. God, being wholly good, perfect, and beautiful, can only appear as what He is. God cannot evidence, manifest, as what He is not. If anything that appears seems evil, imperfect, it is not God, and *it does not exist.* But God *does* exist, and He is all that can appear, be evident, or manifest.

What about the appearances of ugliness, evil, age, dissolution? If these appearances are true, they are Truth. If they are Truth, they are God. If they are God, we must accept an impossible God. We must accept a God who is evil, ugly, aging, and dying. Ridiculous, isn't it? Yet it would have to be true if anything of an evil nature could exist and manifest itself. Evil really *is nothing.* God is Something — and the only Something that can appear or manifest as you, as your entire Being, Body, Life, and experience.

The something which is God cannot appear or manifest as nothing. So that which is appearing before you *is God,* and as God It is entirely beautiful, good, and perfect. Actually, there is nothing appearing before you that is separate from you. Whatever appears is your God-Consciousness presenting just what God knows about Himself.

This God-Consciousness, identified as your Consciousness, includes all of everything that can possibly be you or your experience. You may *seem* to be aware of something other than God; but as God is the *only* Consciousness, you have no consciousness apart from God that can be aware of anything. Knowing that God is the only awareness that can express or manifest as your awareness, it follows that you cannot be aware of anything that is not forever included in and as the Consciousness which is God. With this in mind, ask yourself,

"What consciousness is aware of any discord, ugliness, or evil? Can I perceive anything about my Self that God does not know about His eternal, beautiful, perfect Self? With what mind could I know anything about myself that God did not know *as* Himself? What is my Self other than God-Self identified?"

When the peace of His presence has completely obliterated all misidentification, then, and then only, ask this one all-important question of your Self: "What Mind exists that does *not* know Itself as Perfection, as Beauty formed, active, identified as my Identity?" Remember this: the Mind that answers the question is the same Mind that asks the question. There is no mind outside the Mind that is your Self. All the eternal, changeless beauty of Perfection is constantly expressing itself *as* your Self.

> All that you know, *you are*. All that you see, *you are*. All that appears to your awareness is your Consciousness. All the beauty, all the perfection, all the truth you perceive, you are. For there is one Being, one Consciousness of Being, and that is God, conscious of being you.

7

Chapter VIII

LIFE ETERNAL ///

See P.12
in The Word 63/64

*And this is life eternal, that they might
know thee, the only true God,
and Jesus Christ, whom thou hast sent.*
—*John 17:3*

In the foregoing quotation, there is one little word of great importance which has been largely overlooked. That word is *is*. "This is life eternal" — not "is to become," not a promise of eternal life after death, but eternal Life right here and now.

Who or what is "the only true God, and Jesus Christ" we are exhorted to know? God is eternal, omnipotent, omnipresent Life, and Christ is this God-Life identified, individualized, and *manifest* as the Life of you, of me, and of all. The Christ is God identified, God manifest as the entirety of individual identity. This entirety is complete, including the eternality of Life.

Why have we not seen this before? Because we have been taught that there are a creator and a creation. A creator implies beginning, and a beginning implies an ending. A creation implies birth, and birth implies death. *There is no birth and there is no death.* Regardless of the seeming overwhelming evidence to the contrary, birth and death are not true; they are not truth and have no basis in fact. All the mistaken concepts put together cannot change that which is true, that which is Truth.

That which is true, the truth about Life, was *not* created, did not begin, and cannot end. That which is truth about Life individualized, expressed as the Life of the body, did not appear as birth and cannot disappear as death. What is supposed to live? The body. What is supposed to die? The body. Why? Because it is supposed to have been born. It is supposed to appear at birth.

Anything that appears to have a beginning must appear to have an ending because it is not the eternal truth of that thing. It is only an appearance, therefore it must disappear. To whom does a temporal, material body appear? Actually to no one. There is no one seeing, knowing, or being a temporal life in a temporal body. God is the *All*, the *only One*, and there is no one seeing, being, or experiencing Life but that One. God-Life does not appear at birth in a temporal body that is doomed to disappear. There is no coming or going in God-Life, and there is no appearing and disappearing in God-Life, embodied, individualized, identified as the life of individual body.

It is impossible to perceive fully that Life is supposed to live and die—the body. Again and again, we have declared, "God is eternal life." But this appearance of death has gone right on. Of what use is it to repeat these beautiful truths if they are not evident, manifest, as our entire Life, Being, Body, and experience? Declaring the truth isn't *being* the Truth. It is only when we are consciously aware that we are that very truth we are declaring that Truth, individualized, identified, is manifest as our Life, Mind, Soul, Being, and Body.

Why is all this emphasis being placed upon body? It is because the nature of body has been little understood, and this misunderstanding of what constitutes body has been our greatest stumbling block to full revelation. Some of the greatest spiritual lights have appeared to succumb because of this misconception of body. It is true that body should be recognized as only one aspect of the infinite All; but it is also true that the revelation of omnipresent eternal Life includes the realization of this Life individualized, manifest, embodied.

When life is said to be endangered, threatened, it is always the life *of* the body, the life *in* the body, that is supposed to be in danger of departing *from* the body. Usage has accustomed us to speaking of the life of the body or life in the body. Actually, it is more accurate to realize that life is Life *as* the body. Mind, Soul, Consciousness are indivisibly one, and *as one* they are embodied, manifest as the body.

If Life were merely *in* or *of* the body, it would be possible that Life could be separated *from* the body. But this is impossible, for Life is embodied *as* the body and can never separate or depart from Itself. Never will we perceive that "this is life eternal" until we are aware that this eternal Life is eternally alive, embodied as this eternal Body.

Is Life confined, limited to Its embodiment? No! Life, Mind, Soul, Consciousness are one and the same thing, and this One is infinite, eternal, spaceless, timeless God. Life cannot be measured in terms of time and space. Eternity is now, and infinity is here. Eternal Life is this life, and infinite Life is the life that is here, now, identified as your life.

Is this Life the life of a person? No. There is no person, and Life is God. Life does not personalize Itself. We will never see through this thing of the *appearance* of death into the visible manifestation of eternal Life until we are aware of the truth that Life is infinite, eternal, indivisible, and *impersonal*. It is in the misidentification called a person that all the spurious sense of limitation and separation seems to operate.

It is the *misidentification called a person* that is supposed to be born and that is supposed to die. It is this same misidentification that seems to be limited in time and space, to be subject to all the variableness and vicissitudes of a being separate from God-Being. But remember this:

> Never has the identity that you are been the misidentification called a person. Never have you surrendered your identity.

It is only seeming and only temporary. It is as a pinpoint in infinity, in the eternity of your Being. You are awake and aware of your genuine and only identity *now,* and nothing can hinder you or delay you from being your Self.

There is inherent within each of us the consciousness that the limitations called time and space are false and unnecessary. Every so-called human effort to break these limitations is evidence of this fact. There are countless examples of these efforts. When Columbus sailed into the unknown, when an explorer and pioneer in any field launches forth into hitherto unexplored realms, it is this innate awareness of infinitude challenging the spurious appearance of the limitations of time and space. Today we have the jet planes and the spaceships, all engaged in that same endeavor.

It is this inherent awareness that Life individualized is eternal that causes one to wish to prolong life. The medical profession's constant search for newer and more powerful drugs, more intricate and seemingly successful operations, have, as their basis, the innate but misunderstood recognition that Life is eternal and unlimited.

This is also true about health. Established in our consciousness, though sometimes dimly perceived, is the fact, truth, that health is omnipresent, that perfection is normal and immutable, that Life without limitation is omnipotent. If this were not true, there would be no effort to maintain health or to regain health. So you see, even in the midst of the seeming surrender of identity, the *I* that you genuinely are does continue to exist and assert Itself.

"I am the way, the truth, and the life: no man cometh unto the Father, but by me" (John 14:6). Was Jesus speaking as a person here? No. On the contrary, it was only when all false personal sense was obliterated that he could be consciously aware of being the life, the truth, and the way. What does he mean by the statement that "no man cometh unto the Father, but by me"? His meaning is clear: it is impossible to fully perceive God without experiencing God, even as Jesus was experiencing God to the exclusion of all personal sense. It is by seeing and *being* that same Mind, Life, Soul identified, that was individualized as the Master, that we perceive the Father and the Son to be identical, *the same One*.

In order to elucidate further the truth as revealed here, let us continue with the record of this conversation between Jesus and the disciples:

> If ye had known me, ye should have known my Father also: and from henceforth ye know him, and have seen him. Phillip saith unto him, Lord, shew us the Father, and it sufficeth us. Jesus saith unto him, Have I been so long time with you, and yet, hast thou not known me, Philip? he that hath seen me hath

seen the Father; and how sayest thou then, Shew us the Father?" (John 14:7-9).

Isn't that clear? Here it is plainly stated that God is the only one existing as the *I*, the identity of the one we call Jesus. Here we are told that if we would see, perceive, the Father, we must recognize the Father *as* the Son. Yes, the Father and the Son are identical. The Father is identified *as* the Son—and this identity is you.

"In the beginning was the Word, and the Word was with God, and the Word was God ... In him was life; and the life was the light of men" (John 1:1,4). Of course, there was no beginning. God has always existed, and the Word is God. What is the Word? Right here is the glorious Light. The Word is the expression, the identification of God. The Word has always been with God, and eternal Being is never absent nor separate from Itself; and God identified, expressed, and manifest *as you* has never been separate or absent from this same God-Self.

"In him was life." Yes, in him always has existed the Life that is individualized *as* your life right here and now. It has always existed as the Life identified as your Life, Mind, Soul, Being, and Body. And the Life was the Light, enlightenment, of that which is miscalled man. The enlightenment is your consciousness of eternal Life *as* your Life. Conscious enlightenment is conscious, eternal Life.

To realize enlightenment is to see with the eye that is single, to perceive the Body of Light by the Light that is within. Conscious, eternal Life, Mind, Soul, and Being are one; and as one, they are expressed, individualized, manifested as eternal, imperishable Body.

The Body that has been misidentified as flesh, blood, and other material elements is the Light that is the Life and the Life that is the Light evidencing Its eternal, immutable beauty of perfection.

No man *cometh* unto the Father. There is no man, no person existing who needs to turn, or re-turn, to the Father. The Father and the Son are identical, and you are that Identity.

You are the enlightened One. You are the Light, and there is no darkness. You are the way, the Truth, and the Life. You are the Word, the expression, that is *with* God and that *is* God. You are Life eternal being eternally alive. You are eternal Soul being eternally conscious of the perfection and the beauty of Its Being.

Genuinely, you are God being you, and there is none other.

Chapter IX

No Karma

In most of the religions of the Orient we find the teachings of the law of karma. It is quite generally known that this teaching of karma accompanies the doctrine of reincarnation. According to this belief, the results of the sins of omission or commission during each incarnation are extended into the succeeding incarnation. This karmic belief has been adopted by the western orthodox religions in which it is called the law of retribution. In fact, it is so strongly entrenched in the churches that one is tempted to believe that the Christian Church is largely founded upon this false law.

There are those, both inside and outside the churches, who do not take this belief of retribution too seriously; but unwittingly, they submit to it, calling it the law of cause and effect. Of course, all of us who see clearly enough to be accepting this Ultimate know that there is no such thing as a law of cause and effect. It would seem unnecessary to give any attention to this subject of retribution. Yet it is surprising to discover the seeming hold this falsity maintains until it is entirely obliterated. Again and again we have seen instantaneous realization of perfection occur when the one seeking help suddenly perceived that there was no sin, no past in which sin had taken place, and no sinner—past, present, or future.

Let us now get to the underlying falsity of this whole illusion and dispose of it once and for all. It is unimportant whether it pertains to a so-called former incarnation or to that which is called this life; whether it is supposed to have happened a thousand years ago, last year, last week, or an hour ago. *It never happened.* You weren't in it, and it was never in you.

Where were you when you sinned? Were you ever any place but *here,* right where you are now? The eternal *now,* the omnipresent *here* are all that is known and all that exists to be known. As there is no time, when did you sin? You live and move and have your entire being in the eternal *now.* The Consciousness of your Self, as the very presence of that unblemished One, is the *only* consciousness you have of Being. Only that which is eternally, infinitely true as this One is ever true of you. The One you are now is the same identical One you have always been and will ever be.

What were you when you sinned? Were you someone or something other than that which you are *now?* Where is God in all this? Isn't God the All *as* all? Of course He is. Then who was the sinner? What was the sin? *There is no evil and there is no evildoer.* There is no sin and no one existing

105

who has sinned or is capable of sinning. There is no mind that is conscious of being evil; neither is there any consciousness of evil desires, aims, or purposes. Is there a necessity to atone for something that never happened? Is there a human being, a person existing, who is aware of being or having been evil? No. There is no such person. Indeed, we know that there is *no person at all.*

Does this mean that we should dispense with all self-discipline and indulge in these *appearances* of evil? No, quite the contrary. The desire to be morally good and the effort toward that attainment are laudable. Indeed, it is essential so long as one appears to himself to be a human or a personal being. Even in this, though, sometimes the effort to overcome some false desire makes that very falsity appear to be more real, persistent, and formidable.

Then, too, all of us have known those who have attained some degree of human goodness where that attainment has seemed to result in great self-righteousness. There can be no seeming darkness deeper or more dense than that which appears as self-righteousness. However, this does not alter in the least the fact that these first steps toward the goal of full revelation are desirable and essential. The false sense of self-righteousness can only appear to one who thinks he has attained his goal humanly and stops there.

There are those who have experienced full Self-revelation instantaneously. Even while seemingly immersed in the grossest materiality, this glorious Light has been known to burst through suddenly and reveal the beautiful, pure, perfect Self. But with most of us, this does not happen. It seems necessary for one step to follow the other in the search for this Self. The paradox is that this Self was the only Self that was there at all and the only One who had ever existed *as* the seeming searcher.

> In other words, that which we seem to be seeking, we are.

We are not really seeking It. Rather It is insisting on being Itself *as* us. We have no choice. We cannot escape It, for we cannot escape from ourselves. Even if we desired and tried to suppress this *I*, it would avail us nothing. It is the nature of God to express Himself, and nothing can stop or hinder that expression of Himself as the *I* of each of us.

Yes, even the desire to be humanly good gives us a hint of the irrepressible nature of the Self. What is that which we interpret as the desire to be better? Here again, as in the desire to eliminate time and space, there is within each of us the inherent consciousness that *we are already wholly good*. Furthermore, evil is not only unattractive, but it is also unnatural, unknown, and nonexistent. That which appears as evil *is* unnatural, for it is not inherent in the nature of God. It is unknown because God is the only Mind, and He knows it not. It is nonexistent because God is the All, and God is entirely good. It is unattractive, as it is without existence or power to attract. All of this is known to the Self, and it is this innate knowledge that causes us to resist its seeming imposition.

All desire to improve morally and all effort in that direction are good and natural. But the Ultimate reveals something far greater than this. The Ultimate reveals that which exists rather than that which does *not* exist. It reveals that there was never a past in which we have sinned and that there is no future in which we *become* sinless. In the Ultimate, we know that there is no evil to attract, no one who is or can be attracted to its nothingness, no time when it was, and no time when it will be.

Here there is no retribution, no atonement, and none in need of atonement. Here there is no overcoming or becoming. All *is,* and All is gloriously good and perfect *now.* Here we know that we can never *become* that which we *are.* We also know that never can we *overcome* that which we *are not.* Here there is no consciousness of anything to become or to overcome. Here there is just the awareness of eternal Perfection being eternally, immutably perfect. Here our conscious eternal Being is complete, even to the complete exclusion of any illusion of wrongdoing or a wrongdoer. This All-conscious Being, which is the only Self, is fully aware of changeless beauty, purity, and perfection, not only of Itself, but of all.

Dear reader, it must be clear to you now that there is no law of karma. There is no past, ancient or recent, in which you sinned. There is no memory of something that never happened. There is no present or future retribution or atonement to be made and no one who recognizes or is aware of any such necessity. Actually, there is no time or place. There is no past and no future. There is only *here* and *now.* And you forever abide in this *here and now* in conscious joy, peace, purity, beauty, wholeness, holiness, and perfection. This is you. This is your identity. This is God-Being and God being you.

> There is therefore now no condemnation to them which are in Christ Jesus, who walk not after the flesh, but after the Spirit (Rom. 8:1).

No, there is no condemnation, no self-condemnation and no condemnation of another. There is none to condemn and none to be condemned.

> You are *in* the Spirit *as* the Spirit. You are not condemned — *you are free now.*

Chapter X

LOVE

What is love? God is Love, and there could be no God without Love. Neither could there be Love without God. The Bible says that love is the fulfilling of the law. In the Ultimate, there is no law. What it really means is that Love is God fulfilling His own Being, for Love *is* fulfillment. No truth would be complete without Love. No expression of Truth would be worth listening to or reading if it were without Love. The Life, the Spirit, the fire of the expression are the inspiration of Love.

When you read some inspired message and your consciousness surges upward in joyous response to what you are reading, what is it in the writing that brings this response? Certainly it is not the words. It is the Love which is God pouring forth Itself, and your response is the God-Love *as you*, in glad recognition and acceptance of Its own Truth.

> And it came to pass, that, while they communed together and reasoned, Jesus himself drew near, and went with them ... And it came to pass, as he sat at meat with them, he took bread, and blessed it, and brake, and gave to

them. And their eyes were opened, and they
knew him ... And they said one to another, Did
not our heart burn within us, while he talked
with us by the way, and while he opened to us
the scriptures? (Luke 24:15, 30, 32).

Yes, when Jesus talked *their eyes were opened*
and *their hearts burned within them.* What is it that
opens our eyes and causes our hearts to flame in
joyous response to what we hear or read? *Always*
it is the Spirit, the Love which is God, expressing
Itself *as* the message, the messenger, and the one
responding to the message. Love is infinite and
infinitely expressed. It is indivisible, as Mind,
Soul and Life are indivisible; and the Love that
responds is the same Love that inspires the
message.

Love and Life are inseparable. Love is the Life
of the truth you hear and read. Without Love, the
words are lifeless, uninspiring. Without Love,
there could be no recognition, acceptance, or
response to the message; no communion with the
messenger. You see, the Love that inspires the
message, the Love that *is* the message, and the
Love that responds to the message are the same
Love; just as the Mind that reads the truth is the
Truth as well as the Mind of the one who presents
It.

Everything responds to love. Indeed, love is
essential to life, for without love, life would be
incomplete. Life and love are indivisibly one.

Animals, birds, even plants and flowers respond to love. It is just as natural for a plant to respond to love as it is for its leaves to turn toward the light. We often hear of the proverbial "green thumb" of one who is successful with plants or flowers. The author once asked a friend what she did that caused her plants to flourish. Quick as a flash the answer came: "Oh, I just love them." Yes, love *is* fulfillment.

Just as Life and Mind are impersonal, so is Love impersonal. Sometimes we hear an objection to the word *impersonal* where Love is concerned. This is because impersonal Love is thought to be cold, distant, something separate or apart from us. Nothing could be farther from the truth. The Love which is God, and the Life, Mind, Soul which are God, are one. And as one, they are expressed, individualized, as the identity of each distinct expression. Love can never be cold or distant. It is Love that is the warmth of our entire Being. Who that has experienced illumination has not felt Love, warm and beautiful, surging and flowing as irrepressible Life? No, impersonal Love is never cold or distant. Quite the contrary.

The whole difficulty about this word *love* is in the misinterpretation of it. Love *does* respond to Love, but it is not the love of one person responding to the love of another. The attempt to personalize Love is the attempt to divide, to limit Its illimitable nature. This attempt to limit the limitless, to divide the indivisible, can only bring frustration and disappointment. But the Love which is Its own Self-fulfillment never knows disappointment or frustration.

Love is changeless; Love is constant. It does not love today and stop loving tomorrow or next week. Love must express Itself, and It *is* expressing Itself as the love of individual you and me. But It is not a personal love, and It is not expressed through or *as* a person. As stated before, there is no such thing as a person.

Love never depletes Itself by loving any more than Life depletes Itself by living. Love can never be confined or restricted to person, place, or thing. Does this mean that we are to stop loving and being loved? No. Rather we love with a greater love and are loved with a more perfect love when we know the true nature of love. Actually, we never know the meaning of that word *love* until we experience the impersonal Love which is God.

Just as surely as we exist as Life identified and expressed, we exist as Love. We cannot withhold Love, and Love cannot be withheld from us. It is the nature of Love to give of Itself. There is no such thing as selfish Love. *If it appears to be selfish, it is not Love at all.* Love never seeks to possess. It knows It has all because It is All.

That which we have misinterpreted as being our love for another or the love of another for us is really *the one indivisible Love*. We *are* that Love, and

It *is* fulfilling Itself as the completeness of our experience. It is never absent from Itself, and It is never absent from Itself expressed or individualized. There is no unmanifest Love, and there is no interval in which Love is not manifest.

The one who seems to be seeking Love is the very Love he is seeking. The Love that responds is the same Love with which he loves. In other words, to *know* Love is to *be* Love, and to *be* Love is to know Love. Never reach outside for Love. It is never found outside your own Being. To *know is* to *be* that which is known.

> For I am persuaded, that neither death, nor life, nor angels, nor principalities, nor powers, nor things present, nor things to come, nor height, nor depth, nor any other creature, shall be able to separate us from the love of God, which is in Christ Jesus, our Lord (Rom. 8:38-39).

Nothing can separate us from the Love which is God, for nothing can separate us from our existence. God is Life, Mind, Soul, Love, and God is complete. His completeness fulfills Itself as our completeness.

What has all this to do with so-called human love? Nothing at all. There *is* no human love. There *is* no human being to love or to be loved. That which has been called human love is not Love at all. It is a misuse, a misinterpretation, a misidentification of the Love which exists as the *All.*

In the Ultimate, which is the Only, Love is unfettered, pure, uncontaminated by human longing or human satisfaction. In this Love, human emotions such as jealousy, hate, fear, or selfishness are unknown. Abiding in and as this Love, there is no one outside who can either give or withhold Love. Here there are no impure desires, no emotional upheavals. Here there are no material senses; there is no sensuality. The only Love that exists is pure, untainted, beautiful, and free.

> Yes, God *is* Love. And there is no other love, no other kind of love. The Love which is God is the only Love you can know or experience. *The Love which is God is you.*

Chapter XI

GREATER WORKS

Believe me that I am in the Father, and the Father in me: or else believe me for the very works' sake.

Verily, verily, I say unto you, He that believeth on me, the works that I do, shall he do also; and greater works than these shall he do.

John 14:11-12

What are these greater works we are promised? What does it mean to believe on me? Are we asked to believe on a personal Jesus? No. In fact, there never was a personal Jesus any more than there is a personal you or me. We misunderstand the whole significance of the New Testament if we believe that Jesus, as a person, came forth from God to heal, correct, or improve that which God had permitted to happen. But the Christ *was* here, *is* here, and *will ever continue to be here.*

What is the Christ? God expressing, God individualizing, identifying Himself as you, as me, as all. This is the Christ in which we are asked to believe. This is the "me," the *I* we are invited to accept, recognize, and believe on. We are asked to be aware of the one *I* as the identity of each of us.

This is the Christ to whom the greater works are promised.

Now, you may be asking, "What are these greater works? What could be greater than the works Jesus performed?" Here we begin to arrive at the Ultimate. Here we are indeed on holy ground, for the full revelation is upon us.

> The constant, uninterrupted consciousness of omnipresent, omnipotent Perfection, completely eliminating even the appearance of evil, sickness, sin, sorrow, lack, birth, change, death —this is the greater works, and this is the Ultimate.

This is the goal we have been steadily approaching since we took our first faltering footsteps along the spiritual path. Here in the Ultimate, we know, really *know* that we *are* that which we have been seeking. Here we know our *eternal* identity— perfect, pure, entire, beginningless, changeless, endless. Here there is no becoming, no overcoming. Here even the appearance of evil in any form is *unknown.*

We know that while we seemed to be seeking something outside ourselves, what we were really seeking was to assert our identity in the name of Almighty God. Here no sign, demonstration, healing shall be given, for no sign is needed. There is nothing to heal, nothing in need of change, and no awareness of evil, inharmony of any name or nature.

117

"But," you may be saying, "I haven't arrived at this point." Dear reader, you don't have to arrive; *you are here now*. Never have you been away. You could not possibly exist unless you existed in and as the Consciousness of the Ultimate. When you say, "I AM THAT I AM," you include *where* you are, *when* you are, as well as *what* you are. Nevertheless, for you who still seem to be seeking, the following shall be written.

In searching for a word to replace the misleading term *healing*, we arrive at the word *revelation*. It is true that this word more clearly presents that which takes place when present perfection is realized. It is equally true that there are other words that may throw more light on this subject.

For instance, the words *seeing, perceiving, clarification*, are all helpful. It is best to use the word that means the most to you. However, the use of any of these words is inadequate unless one point is clearly perceived: there is nothing being revealed *to* you. Rather All is being revealed *as* you. There is a marked difference there, you know. As long as it seems that something is revealed *to* you, it also appears that you are separate from that which is perceived. This is dualism. When it is clear that you exist *as* that which is revealed, there is *oneness*.

You are not someone outside waiting for revelation to take place. Revelation is not something outside of you to be sought or found. *You are the revelation*. You are God revealed, and there is nothing going to be revealed *to* you that does not exist *as* you this instant and eternally. In this way, you see perfectly, and seeing perfectly, you see Perfection. In that which has been miscalled healing, this is exactly what has taken place. So again, use the word that enables you to perceive most clearly that you are that which is revealed— that you are the revelation.

The author well remembers a situation when all seemed dark, and in desperation the cry burst forth, "Oh Father, are You here?" Instantly came the glorious response, "If *I* weren't here, you wouldn't be here." In that instant of revelation, the Light dawned. It was seen that there was no darkness and no one in darkness.

This is also true of you and of all. *If God were not here, now, you wouldn't be here*. If God did not exist *as all* of you, it would be impossible for you to exist at all. You have heard that God is "closer than hands and feet." Indeed, He is. God is the hands and the feet, the flesh, the bones, the entirety of your substance and form. And God is Spirit, Consciousness, Love, Life, and Beauty. That which has appeared to be matter is not matter at all. It is simply what God *is*—seemingly misidentified, misperceived.

Now we have arrived at that which has been miscalled healing. Remember, though, that in the Allness of God, there is nothing to be changed,

nothing to be added to, and nothing to be subtracted from omnipresent, omnipotent Perfection.

When you seem to be in need of help or a call
for help comes to you, your immediate response to
this seeming need is important. It must be seen
instantly that there is nothing in need of healing
and no one in trouble. It often happens that this
first seeing is all that is necessary. Frequently the
one who has called reports back at once that all is
well. Again, instantaneous realization of Perfection
may occur during the first telephone call for
help. This often happens. But if there is no
immediate report of realization, something more
is requisite.

The first necessity is to withdraw all attention
from what appears to be the outer world. Be very
quiet and let that "peace that passeth all understanding" take over completely. Sometimes it
helps to take a loved quotation from the Bible
or some other spiritual writing and dwell on it.
Sometimes a statement that has never occurred to
you before will come forth.

Don't try to think—and above all, don't try
to tell God the truth. He already knows it; He
needs no reminder. Be silent. Listen for the truth
that is necessary at the moment to reveal itself.
When all false sense of a human or personal self is
silenced, the *I* in thee has taken Its rightful place—
the *I as* thee. Dwelling in this Consciousness, the
awareness of Being is seen, felt, and known. Then,

and not until then, does that *I*, that Identity, speak, and it speaks *as you.*

Why is all this necessary? Because just so long as that little false misidentity, that little self, claims to be present, the genuine and only *I* that is your God-Being does not speak. And it is when this *I* speaks that "it is done."

How was it that Jesus could reveal instant perfection where imperfection appeared to be? It was because he knew that of himself he was nothing, could be nothing, and could do nothing. But he also knew that as the presence of the power of God, and the power of the presence of God, he could do all things perfectly. He knew his identity as God identified. Furthermore, he knew that the individual standing before him was the same Life, Being, and Body identified. This knowing does not take place so long as there is any sense of being something or doing something of yourself in evidence.

To many who are living almost constantly in and as the conscious Presence, no preparation is necessary because they are already aware of being just what God is and nothing else. But if one is not in this full consciousness of Being, it is necessary to shut everything else out and be silent until this Presence is felt and experienced as the All of Him.

Sometimes we are asked, "Just how do you give a treatment in the Absolute?" No one can answer that question. There is no formula, no set way to approach this subject. Actually, the word *treatment* is not quite right, as it implies someone and something to treat. The word *realization* comes closer to expressing that which takes place. It is the revelation of that which is Truth, fact, actuality, which reveals present Perfection where imperfection had seemed to be. That which reveals Itself is the so-called treatment. This takes place in and as the Consciousness of the practitioner, but that same Consciousness is also the Mind, Soul, awareness of the one who has called for help.

While it is true that there is no formula for treatment, some basic truths concerning this realization may be of help. It is with this in mind that the following is presented.

The first requisite is the conscious awareness of God *in* all, *as* All. This is not something to be declared over and over. It is something to be *felt*. It is God announcing His presence and power as the All of the all. Once this Presence is felt, be still and let God reveal Himself as He will. God is His own Truth and can only reveal Himself *as He is.*

It is when God is *felt* and *known* to be your entirety that you can speak with authority because, you see, then it is not a little human "you" speaking. *It is God revealing Himself.* And you know now that this God-Self is the Self of you, as well as the Self of the one who has called you. There is no separation between you and the one who seems in need. You are the very same

122

Christ-Consciousness: "Christ the power of God, and the wisdom of God" (1 Cor. 1:24). "I live; yet not I, but Christ liveth in me" (Gal. 2:20).

Yes, it is Christ living, alive *as* you and *as* the so-called patient. Christ is God expressed, identified, as you and as each distinct identity. *There is one infinite, all-inclusive God*, and there can be no separation, no division within His infinitude. There is distinction, but not division.

You can perceive from this truth that there is no absent treatment. You are not limited or confined by locality or space. This is equally true of the one who has called upon you. This is why it is possible for one who is apparently halfway across the world from you to instantly realize Perfection where imperfection had appeared to be. You are not separated by either time or space, for there is no such thing as time or space. There is here and there is now. Infinity is *here* and eternity is *now*.

Never attempt to project a treatment or send out a thought. There is no one "out there" to receive it. In fact, *there is no "out there."* This false concept of a "here" and a "there" is dualism. Dualism is not only the illusion that God can be separated into countless parts; it is also the belief that eternity can be separated into measurements of time and that infinity can be separated into measurements of space. It is now becoming known that eternity and infinity are but different

123

terms for the same thing. The leading physicists of today are misinterpreting this truth. Nonetheless, they are beginning to dimly perceive that what they call *time* and *space* are the same thing. As you know, they are attempting to measure space by light-years.

At this point you may be asking, "But what about the body? Isn't each body a separate and distinct entity?" Here again, we return to that word *body* which is the crux of much of the mistaken sense of dualism. To be sure, your body is distinctly identified as *your* body. The same thing is true of the body of the so-called patient. But the thing to remember is this: *it is the same Consciousness embodied as your body and as the body of the one about whom you are realizing present perfection.* God is Consciousness, and Christ is God being conscious of Himself as the Life, Mind, Soul, Being, and Body of each one of us. There is nothing embodied that is not this Christ-Consciousness.

Now can you see how impossible it is for there be such a thing as an imperfect body? The omnipresent Christ-Consciousness is the substance, the form, and the activity, life, of the body. And this is just how far you are, and how far your so-called patient is, from Perfection. The body is *conscious Perfection embodied*. Yes, conscious Perfection being consciously perfect is the only body identified as your body or as the body of anyone.

It must be clear now that the Consciousness revealing Itself as omnipresent Perfection is your Consciousness, as well as the Consciousness of the one you have in Mind, in Consciousness. It is also true that the conscious Perfection *embodied* as your body is the same conscious Perfection embodied as the body of the one who has appealed to you for help. With this realization comes the further revelation that what you are knowing is known as the Mind, Life, activity, being, and body of the one who seemed for a little instant to have surrendered his Identity.

Suppose, for instance, a call should come in and someone were to say, "Work for life." All of us have had that experience. What do you do? How can you work for life? Can anything that you do bring into existence any more of life than already exists? *God is Life*, the *only* Life that lives. There is never any more or any less of God. Neither can there be any more or any less of God-Life living, identifying, as the life of each one of us.

No one lives the Life that is God. Rather it is that God lives His own Life as the Life of each identity. This Life never began, nor can It change or come to an end. This Life didn't start to live as the Life of you or of me, and It can't stop living as the Life of you and all. It has always been and will forever be alive as the Life of each identity. It is never in danger; It is not threatened; It cannot come or go. *It is.* Never can Life be absent from Itself, and this same Life is the Life of your Self. It is also the Life of the Self of the one who is temporarily unaware of It. *The body cannot die because it is this Life embodied.*

There can be no consciousness of death because conscious Life is embodied as the body. There is no consciousness of death in conscious Life. This will give you an inkling as to what reveals itself when some seeming threat to life is presented to you. But don't try to use these words as a formula. God reveals Himself in an infinite variety of ways. What reveals itself tomorrow may be altogether different from that which is revealed today. But you can be assured of one thing: *it will be exactly the revelation that should come for that particular situation.* So always *wait on God.* He is never absent. He is never absent from Himself, and that Self, identified, is your Self.

It is the function of Life to live eternally and perfectly. Life is not an obstacle race to be run. It is the nature of Life to live joyously, freely, triumphantly. Conscious Life knows no impediment, no opposition, no obstacle to Its expression and manifestation of Itself. It fulfills Its nature by functioning as irresistible, irrepressible Life. This is the Life that is evident, manifest, as your Life, as the Life of the so-called patient, and as the Life of all. "Be still, and know that I am God." *I, God will fulfill my nature, my function, and there is none to hinder or to impede.*

Sometimes the false picture presented is that some part or portion of the body, an organ or something like that, is not functioning properly. It is the nature and the function of eternal, infinite Perfection to be eternally, infinitely perfect—not only to be perfect but to remain immutably perfect. *Conscious, perfect Life does not function imperfectly or as imperfection.*

If the body or some portion of it seems to be diseased, deteriorating, or abnormal in any way, the truth of what constitutes body reveals itself. Soul, Life, Consciousness, Mind are the entirety of the body. Conscious Perfection does not change to conscious imperfection. Immutability does not become mutable. Conscious Perfection and Its manifestation are identical. There is not Consciousness *and* manifestation. Consciousness is manifest *as* the Substance, Form, and Life of all that has substance, form and life. There is no false evidence, for there is nothing other than conscious Perfection that can evidence, manifest, or exist. Perfection manifests as what It *is*; It cannot manifest as what It *is not*.

Never be concerned with any appearance of discord. No matter how violent or assertive its pretensions may be, *it just isn't there*. You can't eliminate *nothing*. You can't heal or change something that does not exist. Furthermore, there

127

is no one seeing, perceiving, or experiencing that which is without Life, Mind, substance, activity, or existence. Your only concern is with the revelation of that which *does* exist; and this revelation *always* discloses omnipotent, omnipresent, conscious Perfection being Itself, evidencing as just what It is.

One of the most vicious aspects of the nothingness called evil is the *appearance* of a malignant growth of some kind or other. This pernicious deception is generally accompanied by fear, by an assumptive mind that is afraid. But *Truth reveals Itself as the only Mind*. In this one Mind there is no fear and nothing known to fear. All that is known to Mind is what It knows about and *as* Itself.

Let us not quail before this assumption of nonexistent evil. Let us face it squarely and see through its pretensions. This has nothing to do with affirmations and denials. When we know the truth of anything, we don't go around affirming it and denying its opposite. For instance, we know that white is white; thus we feel no need to affirm it over and over again or to deny that it is black. It has been revealed to us that white is white, and that settles it once and for all.

In the same way, it has been revealed to us that God, conscious Perfection, is all that exists of anyone or anything, and this leaves nothing to affirm or to deny. We just know that *it is,* and that is the entire basis of our knowing.

And Moses answered and said, But,
behold, they will not believe me, nor hearken
unto my voice ...

And the Lord said unto him, What is that
in thine hand? And he said, A rod.

And he said, Cast it on the ground. And he
cast it on the ground, and it became a serpent;
and Moses fled from before it.

And the Lord said unto Moses, Put forth
thine hand, and take it by the tail. And he put
forth his hand, and caught it, and it became a
rod in his hand ...

And the Lord said further more unto him,
Put now thine hand into thy bosom. And he put
his hand into his bosom: and when he took it
out, behold, his hand was leprous as snow.

And he said, Put thine hand into thy
bosom again. And he put his hand into his
bosom again; and plucked it out of his bosom,
and, behold, it was turned again as his other
flesh (Ex. 4:1-4, 6-7).

Whether we believe that this happened or
whether we consider it simply as an allegory is
perhaps not too important. There is tremendous
truth disclosed here for those who have *eyes to see.*

What was Moses' first reaction to the serpent
that was no serpent? To flee in fear; to quail before
it. Why? Because it appeared as something evil
with life, intelligence, substance, and activity —
something destructive. And what happened when
the inner voice of God prompted Moses to turn,

pick it up, and really see what was there? *Revelation.* The truth, fact, of that which really existed was revealed.

Where was the evil? What was the serpent? Where and what was it that assumed life, intelligence, and activity of an evil nature? It didn't exist in or as the rod. One might say that it existed in the mind of Moses. But did it? If it had, Moses would have known that it was real and true; he wouldn't have even attempted to run away from it because he would have known that it was included in and as his eternal existence and thus was inescapable. No, it didn't exist as either the rod or the consciousness of Moses. It didn't exist *as* life, activity, mind, intelligence, or substance. *It didn't exist.*

What happened when Moses really looked at and saw that rod? He saw what was there and what had been there all the way through. He didn't have to deny that there was a serpent there; he knew what *did* exist, and that was all that was required. It was revelation, perception—the Light.

What happened when Moses' hand appeared to become leprous and then appeared whole again? He didn't attempt to flee from this. He simply *looked at his hand again* and perceived that it was just the way it had always been.

Was there any difference in nonexistent evil appearing to be a serpent or appearing to be leprosy? No. In each case, it assumed life, intelligence, mind, and activity to be destructive, harmful; to be something opposed to Life, Mind, Substance, Activity, Being. The only difference is that in the one case evil appeared as something that was outside of Moses that could perhaps be escaped; and in the other, it appeared as a condition of body which was inescapable. Of course, the truth is that there is no evil to appear, either as outside or inside, because God, Good, is all that can appear.

This truth is the nature of that which is revealed to the practitioner when called upon for help. And it is particularly true when nonexistent evil appears to be a parasitical growth of some kind. Its claim has no more validity than had the claim of the serpent or the leprosy. In addition to this, the practitioner sees that there is no one existing that is or can be aware of evil or of any of its pretences.

That which has been called evil does not exist. The only name for it is *nothing*. It is not Life, Soul, or Mind. Evil would claim to be the impossible — absence of Mind. It is ignorance, and ignorance is not power. *Mind, Intelligence, is the only Power, and Mind is omnipresent.* All that Mind ever reveals is the fact of that which already exists. The revelation of this fact is the Power and is unopposed, for there is nothing that can oppose It.

It is the nature and the function of Life to live, and to live eternally. Life is alive *as your life* and is not alive as the life of some parasitical appearance opposed to itself. Anything that seems to be destructive or a threat to life is completely devoid of Life. Evil is lifeless, dead, nonexistent.

There is nothing existing to supply it with activity and nothing to sustain it. It is without form and void. Nothing exists upon which it can feed; and it has no intelligence with which to direct, govern, or maintain itself. Evil is without consciousness, without awareness, and *has no one being consciously aware of its existence.* It is not to be found in all of infinity and eternity. It is unknown to omnipotent, omnipresent Mind and therefore unknown to this Mind individualized, identified as the only Mind of any individual.

> Life lives *as* the life of Itself and as no other life. Mind knows the perfection of Itself, and It knows nothing else. The Truth, known as this Mind, is power because It is the consciousness, the substance, the life and being of that which Mind knows. The Mind that is knowing the Truth is the very substance, form, activity, and life of that which It is knowing.

You are that which you know, and you know what you are. What mind could you be that was unconscious, unaware of itself? What mind could exist that didn't know itself to be the substance, life, activity, and complete existence of all that it knows? This knowing is the conscious awareness of *what you are, when you are, where you are, and why you are.*

Here, you know that you are the very Life, Mind, Soul, Beauty that is eternal God expressed, identified, and manifest *as* you. Here, you know that this is the truth *as* you are now—this instant—and that it is the truth of what you have always been and will ever continue to be. You know also that you live and move and have your being in the kingdom of God, Spirit, and that the kingdom of God is established in and *as* the entirety of your being.

> In addition to this, you know that you *are* because God *is*. You could have no existence unless it were God existing as you. This is the what, the where, the when, and the why of your Being.

You see, it is not within the nature or province of God, eternal Life, to permit a so-called destructive element to live. It is completely contrary to eternal Life to permit the existence of an activity, power, or intelligence destructive or detrimental to Itself. Before there could be such a thing as a disfigured, blemished, diseased substance, God would have to be conscious of it, and He would have to be aware of it as His own substance.

Not only that, He would have to be the disease as well as the diseased substance. He would have to be the substance that was imperfect—the imperfection which was manifest in and as the substance and form—and the mind that knew all this substance, life, form, and activity to be eternally Himself. It is ridiculous, of course, even to consider such things; but would it be, if evil existed and were manifest as substance, form, and activity? No. On the contrary, it would be quite natural, as this is the only way it could be if evil in any form could exist.

Again and again, the author has seen some spurious evidence quickly disappear through just such revelations as these presented here. It may be helpful to you for one or two of these instances to be given.

One false picture presented was of a growth on the face of a member of the family. Instead of seeing something that was not there, the eye was kept single, seeing only what was there. This falsity had been accepted for years and appeared to be growing larger and more vicious. Within just a few days, the whole illusion was dispersed and dispensed with, and that was the end of that.

In another so-called case, an argument of an internal growth was almost instantly silenced by the glorious revelation that such a thing could have no life, mind, or activity because it would have to be God, in opposition to His eternal harmonious Being, if it existed at all.

The revelation and the manifestation are not separate. They are one and identical. No truth can reveal itself without manifesting itself. It is impossible to perceive the Truth without *being* the Truth you perceive. Mind, Consciousness, is all substance, all form and activity. It is this same Mind that perceives Itself as eternally, immutably perfect. The substance, life, and form are conscious, eternal, changeless Perfection manifest.

This explains why the revelation and the manifestation of perfection are simultaneous. How can they be separate when they are identically the same? The "eye that is single" sees all the way. It sees through the mistaken concepts called time and space, through the misidentification called person, through all spurious evidence, to the Perfection which It is.

You need not struggle to become what you eternally are nor strive to overcome what you have never been. As you *are*, you *were*; and as you *are*, you *will be*. Conscious Perfection can never be unconscious of being perfect. God's conscious manifestation of His perfect substance, form, and activity can never be delayed or postponed. It is *now*; It is manifest *now*; It is in action *now*. It is *all* that is in operation, and *all* that is manifest *now*.

God is forever entire, complete. This complete entirety would have to become incomplete if there were a lapse or interruption of His conscious perfection. God is complete, individualized *as* you, as your completeness, as your entirety. If your conscious awareness of eternal perfection were to lapse or be depleted, you would then be incomplete. Your eternal consciousness of omnipresent Perfection is forever included in and as the entirety of your Being.

If God is all that exists (and He is), He must exist *as* all that has existence. If God is all action, Omniaction, He must be the activity of all that acts. Could God, the substance and form of all that is formed, be or become active in or as something that would oppose, obstruct, or in any way hinder His continuous expression of His own perfect Being? Would God form His substance into something that would obstruct His omniaction? The activity, the substance, and the form are all God expressed, and there is no struggle going on in God.

Sometimes the nothingness called evil will attempt to masquerade as a person, or persons, out there with power to disturb, distress, or offend you mentally or emotionally. There is no person out there. There is no personal, mortal, or human mind. There is no mind that has power *over* you. God is the only Mind, and God-Mind is omnipotent *as* you. Any appearance of evil claiming to be the mind of another is entirely false. It is not Mind. It is not Power. *It is not there* because it implies that which is impossible, namely, the absence of omnipresent Mind. Therefore it is ignorance, impotence, nonexistence.

There is no disturbed mind. There is no mind existing that can act as a disturbing factor or influence. There is no evil, unfair, unloving, unjust mind. Neither is there a misunderstanding or a domineering mind. There is no mind withholding anything necessary to your completeness, and there is no mind that can offer or give you anything that will add to the completeness that you are at this instant. There is one Mind, and in the oneness of this Mind there is no division and no separation. There is no mind other than God-Mind that can identify, individualize, and express Itself as the Mind of you, the Mind of me, and the Mind of all. As this Mind, you are eternally conscious of peace, joy, and completeness. Indeed, you are this instant the Mind that is "perfect and entire, wanting nothing."

What about supply? The truth presented throughout this book *is supply*. He who reads and perceives this truth is rich beyond compare. We have been educated to think of supply in terms of money. Nothing could be farther from the truth. Supply includes and is manifest as money, but it is not limited or restricted to just that one aspect. Health and wealth are one and inseparable. God is infinite supply, and God is Life, Truth, Love, substance, form, and *substance formed*.

God would not be complete if any essential were missing from His entirety. God is never absent from Himself. Being All, He is *consciously* All. Indeed, *the very awareness of being All is essential to that Allness, that entirety*. God is eternally, infinitely cognizant of every essential of His Being. The conscious Allness which is God is never unconscious, unaware of being Life, Soul, Mind, activity, health, wealth, beauty, *completeness*.

As stated again and again, you are just what God is, expressed, individualized *as* you. All that God is conscious of being, He is conscious of being *as you*. His consciousness of completeness is your awareness of being complete. There is nothing missing from God identified *as* you. There is no such thing as a lot of God expressed as one and a little of God expressed as another. God is indivisible, inseparable Omnipresence and is equally present as each of us. His completeness is never incomplete, and His expression and manifestation of His allness are never expressed or manifest as incompleteness.

Wealth is indivisible, inexhaustible. Wealth cannot be divided into segments; neither can it be parceled out as either much or little. There is no way of measuring wealth. Can infinity be measured? It is the seeming misunderstanding of what it is that constitutes wealth that causes the false sense of lack and limitation. Perceiving what comprises wealth, we are conscious of a wealth of health, a wealth of life, beauty, love, joy, activity, completeness. No aspect of wealth can be absent or missing, even temporarily, when the totality, the inseparability, of wealth is revealed.

The attempt to demonstrate wealth is futile. It is true that sometimes so-called mental work will apparently produce more money. But frequently, it is only a temporary supply, and at best it is subject to variations and fluctuations. Acquiring wealth in this way, one may be rich today and poor tomorrow. If wealth is considered to be something attained, something gained, it must also be something that can be lost. If it is believed to be separate from you before it was attained, it must also be in the realm of possibility for it to become again separate from you. If it is believed that wealth is possessed, it must also be conceivable that you can be dispossessed of it.

Without the Ultimate perception of what constitutes wealth, there is no permanent, uninterrupted manifestation of wealth. Conscious *seeing* and *being* the very presence of God—infinite, eternal, inseparable Wealth—is the only assurance of Its eternal uninterrupted manifestation. This is true because all that is included in your seeing and being is your Self, and you can never be separate from your Self. Neither can any facet or aspect of your Being be gained or lost, diminished or augmented.

As stated before, money is but one aspect of wealth. In most situations, it seems to be an essential. But suppose for an instant that you were on a raft or lifeboat, adrift on the ocean. Would money then meet the need of the moment? No.

There are many seemingly hopeless situations where money is of no value at all. But there is no illusion of trouble so grave that the conscious awareness of seeing and being the presence of omnipotent God will not bring the revelation that is essential at the moment. This is supply; this is wealth that does not diminish or disappear.

When once the infinite omnipresence of wealth is revealed, there can be no lack, limitation, or poverty. It is from this awareness of what constitutes wealth that the immediate supply for any *seeming* need is realized. Wealth is Consciousness, *your* Consciousness, and you are never absent from your Self. *The manifestation of supply is your Consciousness formed*. It makes no difference what aspect of wealth is the necessity of the moment—whether it is for health, home, money, or whatever—your omnipresent Consciousness can *and does* form Itself into that which meets the need.

You can see from this that *there is no such thing as a need*. How can you need anything that is forever contained within your completeness? There is no separation between the essential and the supply; and there is no separation between the essential and the manifestation of the supply formed into whatever is essential.

If a *seeming* need appears to you, it occurs to your thought. Therefore you are conscious of it. But your Consciousness is the supply, so It cannot really be aware of a need; It can only be conscious of the supply for that which *seemed* to be a need. *The conscious supply existed in and as your Consciousness before the so-called need arose.* In other words, when some apparent need or desire occurs to you, it is just that your attention has been called to the supply that is already existent. If the supply were not already here, that which has been miscalled the need would not have arisen.

That which is essential to your completeness, be it wealth, health, or whatever, is the omnipresent Essential. It is your Consciousness. *If it were not here, you would not be here.* How utterly impossible it is for you to be, even temporarily, separated from that which is established eternally within the entirety of your Being.

Do you remember when we used to declare, "God is my supply," and then wonder how we were going to pay the bills the first of the month? Of course, nothing could be more true than the fact that God is our supply. But it takes more than the mere statement of this truth to realize the continuous, uninterrupted manifestation of supply. The first requisite is the conscious awareness of the infinite Omnipresence as the completeness of your Self.

Money, whether silver, gold, copper, or paper, is not supply. You, your Consciousness is the supply. That which is manifest, evident as money, is simply your Consciousness unfolding, manifesting, appearing in that particular aspect. It is not what it appears to be at all, in the same way that the body is not the kind of body it appears to be. *There is no matter, either as money or body.*

It is the misidentification of that which is money that causes the difficulty. It is this same misidentification that makes it appear as temporal, divisible, unevenly distributed, and something that can be acquired and lost. In this false sense, it also seems as though it could be depleted or augmented, appearing or disappearing. There can appear to be an undersupply or an oversupply, although this latter state may seem impossible to some. Nonetheless, there is such a thing as someone seeming to have too much money when there is no apparent consciousness of what it is or what is best to do with it.

Mind is the substance and the form of money, and Mind is inexhaustible. There is never a shortage of Mind. Neither is there an absence of Mind in manifestation. Mind is Omnipotence, therefore It is the Power manifesting Itself as the substance, form, and activity of all that has substance, form, or activity. Call it idea, evidence, manifestation, or anything you like; the name for It is not too important, just so long as you are aware that It is God, active and producing Himself as that aspect of wealth which we call money.

The Mind that is God is identified, individualized, and expressed eternally *as you*. There is nothing absent or missing from this Mind *identified as your Mind*. Consciousness and Mind are identical. They are One. If any essential could be lacking from the Consciousness that is you, it would mean that God, Mind, Consciousness, was incomplete, absent from Himself.

It is surely clear now that you are entire, complete, eternally, and that you are never for an instant separate or apart from all the wealth, health, joy, and peace you could ever desire.

CHAPTER XII

SEEING IS BEING

Therefore speak I to them in parables: because they seeing see not; and hearing they hear not, neither do they understand.

And in them is fulfilled the prophecy of Esaias, which saith, By hearing ye shall hear, and shall not understand; and seeing ye shall see, and shall not perceive ...

But blessed are your eyes, for they see: and your ears, for they hear.

Matthew 13:13-14, 16

What does it mean to see and perceive? The significance of this is clear. We see by perception. Conscious awareness is perception, and to be consciously aware of the Truth is to see, perceive, the Truth. As we exist *as* Consciousness, perception is inherent in our existence. This is what is meant when someone speaks of seeing with "the eyes of the Soul."

While it is wonderful to know this, yet the Ultimate discloses further revelation:

The Consciousness that perceives the Truth is the very substance, form, and activity of that which It is perceiving.

It is exceedingly important that this be realized. Why? Because to know the truth about the Truth just isn't enough. We have done too much of that already. So often we hear someone say, "Oh, I just knew the truth about it." And all too frequently, the realization of perfection is delayed.

To know the truth *about* something is to feel a false sense of separation between what we are knowing and what we are *being*. This has been one contributing factor to the seeming gap between the truth we were knowing and the Perfection we were seeking to realize. There can be no such gap when it is clearly seen that *the Consciousness that perceives includes that which is perceived.* Knowing Truth in this way, there is no separation between the revelation and the manifestation of that which is revealed.

There is nothing outside your Consciousness that can reveal Itself. To *see* is to *be* what is seen. Comprehending this discloses *seeing as being, revelation as manifestation, one and simultaneous.* This is what takes place when we realize omnipresent Perfection instantaneously. Does this seem obscure to you? Does it seem startling? If so, it is well to ask some questions of your Self.

Isn't God the only Mind that knows? Does He know anything outside His infinite entirety? Does anyone or anything exist in a relative position to God? Isn't God the very substance, form, Soul,

Life, and activity of all that He knows? Is there a consciousness apart from God that can identify itself as my consciousness or the consciousness of anyone? Is there a person or a personal mind excluded from God-Consciousness?

Is God-Mind separated into countless other little minds? Can God-Consciousness be omnipresent as the Consciousness of one identity and not be omnipresent as the Consciousness of another? Isn't God aware of being the entirety of all He perceives? Can anything be revealed to me that is not already included in and as God-Consciousness? If it is included in and as God-Consciousness, can it be excluded from the Consciousness that I am? As God is the only Consciousness that can be individualized, what Consciousness exists that is not aware of being the substance, form, and activity of all It perceives?

When you ask such questions as these of your Self, wait quietly for the answers to be revealed. Make no effort to answer them by reasoning; revelation never appears by reasoning. Know that the answers are inherent in and as your Being, and they will reveal themselves. This revelation is the Self revealed to the Self.

How do we know we exist? By perception, by consciousness, by conscious awareness of being. With what consciousness are we aware of our existence? God is the only Consciousness. *The Consciousness of existence and the existent are one and the same thing.* They are identical. Our seeming mistake has been the illusion that there was Consciousness *and* Life, Consciousness *and* substance and form. Genuinely, there is only One, and that is Consciousness. It is Consciousness *as* Life, substance, form, and activity.

God sees by perception, by consciousness, and God *is* what He perceives. As you are God- Consciousness being conscious, you also see by perception, and *you are what you perceive.* Furthermore, as God is aware of being that which He perceives, so *you* are aware of being that which you perceive. This awareness is without limitations or restrictions. It certainly is not confined to body, but it includes body. If Consciousness did not include body, It would be incomplete. Actually, the perception is the substance, form, and activity of the body it perceives.

Someone has said, "What thou seest, that thou beest." A tremendous truth was realized by the one who said this. God *is* Consciousness and God *is* All. Nothing or no one exists in a relative position to God. In order to exist at all, one *must* exist *as* God-Consciousness. In order to be conscious, one *must* be conscious *as* God-Consciousness, for there is no other. God can have no awareness of a separation between that which He is and that which He knows, because the *consciousness of knowing is the Consciousness of Being.*

You are God-Consciousness expressed, individualized, and you perceive *as* that Consciousness and no other. As God-Consciousness identified, you can perceive in no other way than the way God perceives. If you exist at all—and you do—you must exist as God knowing, God being, God existing. Otherwise, there would be no you.

Actually, you know as God knows, you see as God sees, you act as God being active, and you are conscious as God being conscious.

You perceive your Self to be the substance, form, and activity of all that is included in your perception because your perception is God perceiving; your consciousness is God being conscious. *Your very Being is God being you.*

Chapter XIII

THY NAME

Fear not ... I have called thee by thy name; thou art mine.

When thou passest through the waters, I will be with thee: and through the rivers, they shall not overflow thee: when thou walkest through the fire, thou shalt not be burned; neither shall the flame kindle upon thee.

Even every one that is called by my name: for I have created him for my glory, I have formed him; yea, I have made him.

Bring forth the blind people that have eyes, and the deaf that have ears.

Ye are my witnesses, saith the Lord, and my servant whom I have chosen: that ye may know and believe me, and understand that I am he: before me there was no God formed, neither shall there be after me.

One shall say, I am the Lord's; and another shall call himself by the name of Jacob ... I am the first, and I am the last; and beside me there is no God.

Isa. 43:1-2, 7-8, 10: 44: 5-6

Dear reader, what is thy name? What is your identity? What name other than the *One* could establish your identity? I AM is your name. It is I AM that is established as your identity. When all

149

seeming misidentification is obliterated, the I AM that you are shows forth crystal clear, and you know your Self *as* you are, as you have always been, and as you ever will continue to be. Whereas you were, or seemed to be, blind, now you see.

Of course, there are some who still seem to prefer to be "called by the name of Jacob." For yet a little while, they will cling to the misidentification, the sense of a personal identity, but it doesn't matter, for "they shall all know me, (the only Identity) from the least of them unto the greatest" (Jer. 31:34).

Do you remember the fears and limitations of the misidentification named Moses? When he was faced with the task of freeing his people from bondage, his first reaction was one of self-disparagement. "And Moses said unto God, Who am I, that I should go unto Pharaoh, and that I should bring forth the children of Israel out of Egypt?" (Ex. 3:11).

All self-depreciation, self-condemnation, limitations, restrictions are seemingly inherent in the misidentity, *which is no identity.* It was when Moses realized that he was that I AM that he went forth with confidence, with faith, in his ability to accomplish what had seemed impossible to his mistaken sense of identity. The same thing is true of all of us. In the name, identity, of Almighty God, we can do all things.

Indeed, God has "called thee by thy name." God has identified Himself as you. "Thou art mine." You do not belong to yourself; you belong to God, and of yourself you are nothing, have nothing, know nothing. As God expressed, you are All, have all, perceive all. In this perception, there is no fear and no danger threatens. Here there is nothing destructive, harmful, or evil. Here you know that God has identified Himself as you, has given you His name, I AM. You have not chosen God; He has chosen you. He has chosen to evidence, manifest, His glorious Being *as* you. "Ye are my witnesses"—you are the evidence that *I* am, and there is no other *I.*

Who or what is the God that has chosen you? It is your Self, your God-Self, insisting upon being Itself *as* you. The inner response you feel is Self-revelatory. It is your Absolute Identity in Self-recognition. As your Self, you know as you are known, and eternal, beginningless, changeless, endless, conscious perfection is perceived to be your entirety. Seeing the Light by being the Light, Self-recognition is complete. Self-revelation is Self-illumination. You are the Light, and in you there is no darkness at all.

Now you can see what the Master perceived when he declared, "I am the truth, the life, and the way," for you also are the truth, the life, and the way. This instant, you stand in your entirety as all the Truth and all the Life and Mind that has been

151

presented in the Ultimate. "And the way, ye know" because your conscious Identity is the way.

Go forward in the Light *as* the Light, for you are the very brightness of His glory. He has identified Himself as you. He has given you His name, I AM. You are free and you know it. You are not under the law, for you are the principle of your own Being.

> You are the I AM that is Self-governed, Self-sustained, and Self-maintained throughout eternity and infinity. This is the Absolute; this is the Ultimate; this is you.

Chapter XIV

THE ULTIMATE

*And I saw a new heaven and a new earth:
for the first heaven and the first earth were
passed away; and there was no more sea ...*

*And I heard a great voice out of heaven
saying, Behold, the tabernacle of God is with
men, and he will dwell with them, and they
shall be his people, and God himself shall be
with them, and be their God.*

*And God shall wipe away all tears from
their eyes; and there shall be no more death,
neither sorrow, nor crying, neither shall there be
any more pain: for the former things are passed
away.*

Rev. 21:1, 3-4

By many, these verses from Revelation are considered to be a prophecy that heaven will
appear in some distant future. Nothing could be
more misleading than this misconception of the
truth as stated here. This is no prophecy. This is
revelation, and what it reveals is the kingdom of
God right here and now. This is not the way it
shall be; it is the way it has eternally been and will
forever continue to be. Seeing the Light by being
the Light, we know this to be true.

We do not struggle to become what we already are or strive to attain a kingdom that is eternally here. The tabernacle of God is within each of us because God expresses Himself as all of us. There shall no longer be even the appearance of sickness, sorrow, or death, for the seeming surrender of our identity has dissolved in the glorious Light of the Ultimate.

You are no longer a seeker after the Light. Rather it is that you are the Light Itself, rejoicing in Its own Self-perception. Here you stand in the Light, as the Light, constantly expanding in Self-revelation.

Now you know that you have never surrendered your identity, have never been other than you are at this instant. You are fully aware of your Absolute Identity *as* God identified. You are conscious of the glory you had with Him before the world began. Here and now, there are no fetters, restrictions, or limitations; neither are there imperfections to be overcome or problems to solve. Glorious and free, you are established as the eternal Light, glowing, expanding, illuminating your universe. Here, words come to an end.

> Beloved, this is God's gift to Himself. This is your entirety, wholeness, totality, and completeness. This is your Truth, your Life, Mind, Consciousness, Soul, Being and Body. This is *you*. Accept this gift of Self-revelation and rejoice.

About the Author

During early childhood, Marie S. Watts began questioning: "Why am I? What am I? Where is God? What is God?"

After experiencing her first illumination at seven years of age, her hunger for the answers to these questions became intensified. Although she became a concert pianist, her search for the answers continued, leading her to study all religions, including those of the East.

Finally, ill and unsatisfied, she gave up her profession of music, discarded all books of ancient and modern religions, kept only the Bible, and went into virtual seclusion from the world for some eight years. It was out of the revelations and illuminations she experienced during those years, revelations that were sometimes the very opposite of what she had hitherto believed, that her own healing was realized and that this book, *The Ultimate*, came.

During all the previous years, she had been active in helping others. Since *The Ultimate* was published, she has devoted herself exclusively to the continuance of this healing work and to lecturing and teaching.

To all seekers for Light, for Truth, for God, for an understanding of their own true Being, *The*

Ultimate will serve as a revolutionary and wholly satisfying guide.

Revelations continued to come to her from within her own consciousness, and these she set forth in her book, *You Are the Splendor,* and many others.

Made in the USA
Columbia, SC
20 May 2017